PENGUIN PASSNOTES

*Great Expectations*

Jill Talbot was educated at Hove County School and
Leeds Training College. She has recently retired
from the teaching profession. For twenty years she
taught English and has had wide experience of
preparing students for the G.C.E. O-level Language and
Literature examinations. She now lives in Brighton
where she works as a writer, mainly in the ed̶ ̶
field.

PENGUIN PASSNOTES

CHARLES DICKENS

# Great Expectations

JILL TALBOT

ADVISORY EDITOR: STEPHEN COOTE, M.A., PH.D.

PENGUIN BOOKS

Penguin Books Ltd, Harmondsworth, Middlesex, England
Penguin Books, 40 West 23rd Street, New York, New York 10010, U.S.A.
Penguin Books Australia Ltd, Ringwood, Victoria, Australia
Penguin Books Canada Limited, 2801 John Street, Markham, Ontario, Canada L3R 1B4
Penguin Books (N.Z.) Ltd, 182–190 Wairau Road, Auckland 10, New Zealand

First published 1984
Reprinted 1985, 1986, 1987

Made and printed in Great Britain by
Richard Clay Ltd, Bungay, Suffolk
Filmset in Ehrhardt

*The publishers are grateful to the following Examination Boards for
permission to reproduce questions from examination papers used in
individual titles in the Passnotes series:*

*Associated Examining Board, University of Cambridge Local Examinations
Syndicate, Joint Matriculation Board, University of London School
Examinations Department, Oxford and Cambridge Schools Examination
Board, University of Oxford Delegacy of Local Examinations.*

*The Examination Boards accept no responsibility whatsoever for the
accuracy or method of working in any suggested answers given as models.*

# *Contents*

# To the Student

This book is designed to help you with your O-level or C.S.E. English Literature examinations. It contains a synopsis of the plot, a glossary of the more unfamiliar words and phrases, and a commentary on some of the issues raised by the text. An account of the writer's life is also included for background.

The page references in parentheses refer to the Penguin Classics edition, edited by Angus Calder.

When you use this book remember that it is no more than an aid to your study. It will help you find passages quickly and perhaps give you some ideas for essays. But remember: *This book is not a substitute for reading the text and it is your response and your knowledge that matter.* These are the things the examiners are looking for, and they are also the things that will give you the most pleasure. Show your knowledge and appreciation to the examiner, and show them clearly.

# Introduction

## THE LIFE AND BACKGROUND
## OF CHARLES DICKENS

The Penguin copy of *Great Expectations* begins with a brief factual account of Charles Dickens's life and works. The purpose of this introduction is not to repeat what has already been said, but to select biographical and historical background which has direct or indirect bearing on the book and which will add to your enjoyment of it.

For a family trying to keep up appearances, it seems strange that John Dickens's eldest son should have been named after the skeleton in his wife's cupboard. Charles Barrow, Dickens's grandfather, had stolen almost £6,000 and to avoid the disgrace of a prison sentence had fled to the Continent by the time Charles Dickens was born. Angus Wilson believes that such a highly emotional event in the family circle would have been told over and over again and that it provided Dickens with real life experience for Magwitch's escape (see *The World of Charles Dickens*, Penguin Books). In contrast, John Forster, Dickens's friend and biographer, tells of the happy day when Dickens and his companions made the same journey down the river that Pip and Magwitch were to make in their escape bid. Dickens's perception would have missed nothing, and with such stimulating starting points no wonder chapter 54 is so exciting.

Any biography is certain to include the two most traumatic events of Dickens's life: the humiliation of the blacking factory and the disgrace of the Marshalsea Debtors' Prison. The sickening shame of both seeped to Dickens's innermost being, penetrating the depths of his writing and haunting him for the rest of his days.

Dickens became ashamed of home and disgusted with his parents once the carefree Chatham days were over. His father lived beyond his means and each time they moved house they went down in the world. Little by little all their possessions, except the barest minimum, were sold. The Debtors' Prison and the blacking factory loomed before him.

When he was twelve years old, Dickens came to the darkest time of his life. He was sent out to work at the blacking factory 'with common men and boys' to earn a pittance of six or seven shillings a week. Of that time he said, 'No man's imagination can overstep the reality.' He meant the reality of his profound anguish and desolation as he covered enormous quantities of pots of paste-blacking which would later be used to clean the boots of gentlemen. Dickens, 'a small bundle of shivers', was overwhelmed by the hopelessness of the blacking factory for, until that cruel introduction, he had never before known absolute despair.

He had just managed to cope with his London sorrows until then: sorrows caused by living in a neglected area, being lonely, even the emotional trips to the pawnbroker's and parting with his beloved Chatham books. But he had never experienced such excruciating mental pain as the despondency and feeling of abandonment he suffered in the blacking factory.

Once he had been so sure his life would be a success, and he had already reaped applause and praise. He had been a social success at Chatham, entertaining with his comic songs and storytelling. He was a compulsive reader who easily assumed the identities of various characters in stories; he was showing rare ability at school; he had been caught up in the magic of the theatre. Not only had he revelled in the world of make-believe but also in the actuality of beautiful places, roaming the woods and meadows, walking Pip's marshes and sailing up and down the river. He had often stood outside Gad's Hill Place dreaming of the day he would live there.

His father had encouraged that dream by telling him that if he worked hard such a mansion could be his. Thus, Dickens had been untroubled by the financial problems that beset his family in those early, happy days. Not once was there a real hint that it would all end in catastrophe: the soul-destroying blacking factory for him, the Debtors' Prison for his father. It seemed that, like Pip, Dickens's own 'great expectations' were to come to nothing.

Dickens's persistent, obsessive interest in prisons began with the imprisonment of his father in the Marshalsea. When Pip arrives in London one of his first sights is Newgate and later, after he has visited it (p. 284), he feels contaminated. Throughout the novel, Pip is haunted by the 'taint of prison and crime' (p. 284). Dickens's horror and the shame of his painful experiences found an outlet in Pip's. The dreadful days of Dickens's childhood had much to answer for, but the consequences could have been far worse. Being left to his own devices and answerable to no one, he realized later how easily he too might have become a criminal. 'No advice, no counsel, no encouragement, no consolation, no support from anyone . . .'

*Great Expectations* is not autobiographical in the way that *David Copperfield* is, but various episodes and emotions from Dickens's life, as already illustrated, contributed to it. It is generally supposed that Ellen Ternan was in his mind when he put words of love into Pip's mouth and made him address Estella (e.g. p. 378). Dickens fell helplessly in love with this young actress, but the full truth of their relationship remains a mystery. She was young enough to be his daughter, but in her company he felt rejuvenated and exhilarated. He loved her, because he 'found her irresistible . . .' He loved her 'against reason, against promise, against peace, against hope, against happiness, against all discouragement that could be' (pp. 253–4).

*Great Expectations* was originally published as a serial in *All the Year Round*, a magazine edited by Dickens. Because the magazine was losing readers Dickens decided to try and entice them back with this story of mystery, suspense and great excitement. He ended each instalment on a highly dramatic note (the stars at the ends of chapters throughout the text indicate serial breaks) that compelled his readers to come back for more each week.

Charles Dickens had the opportunity to stand for Parliament but although he cared desperately about social reform, he had no political axe to grind. His constituency was the whole world, his policy the dignity of human beings. He abhorred the impersonal machinery of a state fuelled by the evil power of wealth, and in his writing he championed the cause of its victims who were defenceless, dehumanized, degraded, demoralized, and deflated – victims powerless to help themselves.

Dickens's exceptional sensitivity expressed itself through his characters who were based on real people, and much of his own vitality and experience flowed through their veins. In many powerful passages he exposed the exploiters and tyrants for the impostors they were, ridiculing the pompous, deriding the insensitive and creating caricatures of all those who had ceased to be human. He promoted the underprivileged whom society had cast aside, eliciting a sympathetic response from his readers, and communicating warmth and kindness to those he supported.

# *Synopsis of* Great Expectations

*Great Expectations* consists of three stories woven into one, each with its own main characters – Pip, Miss Havisham and Magwitch – and each with great expectations as the common theme. Some characters appear in all three stories, and this may confuse the student new to Dickens.

You will find Pip's story easier to follow if we begin this section with the chronological order of events; then, as you read the novel again, you will be able to make sense of the plot and enjoy the ingenious way all the parts combine. Let us look first at Magwitch's story.

## Magwitch's story

This might almost be called the Magwitch mystery. It began when his father deserted him (p. 360) and he became a juvenile offender. His relationship with a woman named Molly resulted in a child whom Magwitch loved (p. 406). However, Molly was 'a wild beast' and, in a fit of passionate jealousy, she murdered another woman who had had an affair with Magwitch. Molly was just as likely to kill their three-year-old child and, because he believed that she had done so, Magwitch made himself scarce at her trial. In spite of her horrendous crime and the way she treated him, Magwitch felt compassion for Molly, and the last thing he wanted was to give evidence in court (either about the child or the woman) that would result in Molly's death (p. 418).

Jaggers made his name defending Molly and, although in hiding, Magwitch followed the course of events with interest. That was the last he heard of Molly, and he believed his child was dead.

Just before this 'dark wild part' (p. 417) of his life, Magwitch had met Compeyson at Epsom races (p. 361). Compeyson took him on as a partner and then masterminded whatever illegal business he could think of for making money. He had a hold over Magwitch because he knew that Magwitch had been an accessory after the fact, lying low at Molly's trial in order to avoid incriminating her (p. 419).

When eventually they were both arrested and convicted, Compeyson, the 'gentleman', had everything on his side. This raised him high above Magwitch in the judge's estimation and, compared to Magwitch's, his was a lenient sentence (p. 365). Magwitch swore revenge but it was some time before his opportunity came and when it did, guards quickly isolated him on the prison-ship (p. 366). He escaped to the marshes where Pip came upon him, and the story begins, on that fateful Christmas Eve (p. 36).

Magwitch learns from Pip that Compeyson is free too. He tracks him down, keeping his promise of revenge, and then hands him over to the soldiers, thus sacrificing his own chance of escape (p. 67). Again Compeyson receives better treatment. Excuses are made on his behalf, but there is no mercy for Magwitch. He is transported to Australia for life (p. 366).

Within ten years Magwitch has made a fortune in New South Wales. He has inherited money from his employer, gained his freedom and worked with the great expectation of making Pip a gentleman. He had been so impressed when the young lad had stolen food and a file without betraying him, and so incensed by the system that favoured Compeyson, that he vowed he would make a 'gentleman' of his own. The only lawyer he knows is Jaggers, so he sends his legacy and first profits to London with the instructions that Pip receives in the state parlour (p. 165).

As for Molly, guilty though she was, Jaggers got her acquitted. He made a bargain and promised to do his best for her if she would hand over her child for adoption (p. 425). He needed the child for a rich client, and he told Molly that whichever way the verdict went the child's safety was assured. So at the age of three Molly's child went to live with Miss Havisham. Her name was Estella. Murder and the fear of death affected Molly. Jaggers took her in, tamed her and she became his housekeeper. It is important to note that, although Estella appears to be a 'lady' throughout the novel, her origins were far more lowly and disreputable than Pip's.

*Miss Havisham's story*

Miss Havisham's story is a melodrama. She was the spoilt child of a wealthy brewer (p. 203). Her half-brother Arthur, a ne'er-do-well, had been disinherited, but on his deathbed the father weakened and left the boy a considerable fortune, although not as much as he left his daughter. No love was lost between Miss Havisham and Arthur, and he blamed her for their father's treatment of him (p. 205).

In league with Compeyson, Arthur got his revenge by working out a wicked ploy to make money. Compeyson was to 'fall in love' with Miss Havisham. He took her to all the fashionable places and lied about his feelings for her. She fell for him so completely however that she was deaf to anyone (especially Matthew Pocket) who warned her against Compeyson.

Compeyson persuaded Miss Havisham to part with huge sums of money, and to buy her brother out of his share in the brewery, promising that when they were married he would run it profitably. Miss Havisham was so blindly in love that she played right into Compeyson's (and Arthur's) hands.

The wedding day came, but the bridegroom did not. Instead a letter arrived shattering all Miss Havisham's hopes and breaking her heart. Her normal life ended at twenty-to-nine. She imprisoned herself, dressed as for her wedding, forever. Her great expectation, thereafter, was to revenge herself on the entire male sex (pp. 200, 321) and to that end she needed a daughter. By now Jaggers was her lawyer and she asked him to find her one to adopt (pp. 412, 425). He produced Magwitch's, telling Miss Havisham that Estella was an orphan.

Arthur drank himself to death. He suffered delirium and died during one of these attacks (p. 363).

*Pip's story*

By putting his hero immediately into the hostile environment of the Magwitch story, Dickens launches his plot with more than the usual suspense and excitement.

Pip, an orphan, living at the forge with his sour sister and gentle brother-in-law, instantly engages our sympathy and interest. The first seven chapters portray his childhood and are dominated by his encounter with the convict, the theft forced upon him and his constant fear of discovery. The one bright feature of his life is Joe's friendship. Pip looks forward to becoming Joe's apprentice.

That is before Pip's visit to Satis House. Miss Havisham, dressed as a bride, yet shrunken and old with her hand on her broken heart, commands him to amuse her, but he cannot. Estella condescendingly plays cards with him. This proud, beautiful girl inspires immediate dreams of gentility and wealth in Pip. He bitterly resents the injustice of the working-class background that allows his 'vulgar appendages' (p. 92). His hilarious account of the visit has poignant undertones as Pip feels unable to explain that he was afraid of Miss Havisham and ashamed of his commonness at this turning point in his life (p. 95 f). He decides to improve himself with Biddy's help (p. 102).

The next time he goes to Satis House, the pale young gentleman (Herbert) challenges Pip to a fight (p. 119). He also meets Jaggers on the stairs. Both Herbert and Jaggers will play a prominent part in his life. But, for the moment, all Dickens provides us with are hints and suspense. This suggestion of a detective story is important to Dickens's dramatic effects.

At fourteen, Pip is apprenticed to Joe and his regular visits to Satis House come to an end. He still yearns to be a gentleman and good enough for Estella. He despises Joe's trade and fears the shame of being caught at his common task by Estella or Miss Havisham. About a year later he returns to Satis House. Miss Havisham takes spiteful pleasure in telling him that Estella is 'educating for a lady', and asks if Pip feels he has lost her (p. 144). When he returns to the forge, Pip discovers that Mrs Joe has been savagely attacked.

The Magwitch mystery is revived by the discovery of a convict's leg-iron beside Mrs Joe's body and Pip blames himself for providing the weapon. Nothing is proved against anyone. Mrs Joe's condition grows worse and Biddy becomes housekeeper (p. 150).

Pip confides his secret ambitions to Biddy (p. 154) but he ignores her advice and her love, believing that Miss Havisham will conjure up a fortune for him and he will win his princess. Dickens is showing us Pip's growing snobbery.

When Jaggers brings the astonishing news about his legacy (p. 165), Pip's dream comes true. In the busy week before his departure for London, Pip has personal experience of the 'stupendous' power of money (p. 178 f). His behaviour towards Biddy and Joe is insufferable, but he has regrets at the finger-post, and sheds tears of shame (p. 186). This marks the end of the first third of the novel. We have watched a delightful child become a snob and lose his sense of reality through great expectations which are never truly fulfilled.

London is not the city of bright lights that Pip had anticipated. Almost immediately, he faces disillusionment. Wemmick (Mr Jaggers's clerk) takes him to his temporary lodgings with Mr Pocket in the shabby chambers of Barnard's Inn. He cheers up considerably with the arrival of Mr Herbert Pocket (p. 198) because he recognizes him as the pale young gentleman of the Satis House days. They form an immediate friendship and during their first meal Pip (now nicknamed Handel) hears as much of Miss Havisham's life-story as Herbert knows (p. 203).

Herbert's father, Matthew, is to be Pip's tutor so they travel to Hammersmith to meet him and his extraordinary family and fellow students (p. 209 f).

Some weeks later, Pip accepts Wemmick's invitation to call at Walworth Castle (p. 229) where he is amazed to discover an altogether different Wemmick from the one he had met in Jaggers's office. This is the beginning of a relationship in their 'private and personal capacities' (p. 405). Soon Pip and his companions are invited to Jaggers's house and, on Wemmick's advice, Pip studies his housekeeper (p. 224). There is something odd about her face and wrists (pp. 235, 236) but Dickens keeps us guessing, as a part of his masterly plot development.

Pip's delusions of grandeur have severed him from his homely roots, so that when he hears that Joe proposes a visit his reaction is callous: 'If I could have kept him away by paying money, I certainly would have paid money' (p. 240). Joe bears a message saying that Estella would be glad to see him. Once Joe has gone, Pip reproaches himself for his lack of warmth but his remorse, although sincere, is shortlived. He arranges to visit Satis House without delay.

When we have almost forgotten it, Dickens revives the Magwitch mystery by putting two convicts on the same coach as Pip (p. 248 f) and they take the edge off his excitement about seeing Estella again. Once inside Satis House all the fairy-tale unreality possesses him again. Estella is more beautiful than any woman he has ever seen, but 'what was it' about her that perplexes him? Dickens keeps the mystery alive (p. 259).

In spite of Estella's warning that she has no feeling in her heart,

Pip vows to love her with every fibre of his being, just as Miss Havisham has encouraged him to do (p. 261). There is no room for Joe in Pip's life now, because he is too common for Estella.

Herbert has always known Pip's feeling for Estella but now he warns him against the relationship (p. 271). Pip confesses that he cannot control his emotions.

Later, a letter from Estella directs him to meet her coach and, while he waits, he visits Newgate (p. 280). The prison brings Magwitch to mind again and when Estella arrives Pip is puzzled by 'the nameless shadow' and later by the strange feeling that comes over him (passing Newgate, p. 289) as he accompanies her to Richmond.

What is the connection between Estella, Newgate, his convict, and Jaggers's housekeeper? Pip is thoroughly enmeshed in the Magwitch mystery and it seems to be overlapping Miss Havisham's story. (See p. 367, too, first paragraph of ch. 43.)

Pip becomes an idle spendthrift and he and Herbert are soon in debt (p. 292). When Mrs Joe dies and Pip returns to the forge for the funeral he scolds Biddy for not keeping in touch; he promises Joe that he will be down 'soon and often' (pp. 303–4). Biddy knows that he will not.

Pip grows more reckless and sinks deeper into debt, but when he is twenty-one his allowance is increased (p. 307). He is thus able to help Herbert anonymously and enlists Wemmick's assistance to do so (pp. 313–14).

Meanwhile, Estella and Pip are often together but Pip is never happy in her company. It really is true that she has no feelings and even Miss Havisham becomes a victim of her own scheme when she tries to draw some love to herself (p. 322). Estella has none to give, yet still Pip believes that he has only to wait.

On a wild, desperate night, Magwitch reappears and shatters all his illusions by declaring that he is Pip's benefactor (p. 336). Magwitch's arrival and revelation mark the end of the second stage of Pip's expectations. We have watched Pip grow more arrogant in his false role, but now that Magwitch, the creator of Pip's illusion, has declared himself, the stage is set for Pip's moral recovery. But it will take some time.

There is no disguising the convict's delight at seeing his gentleman, nor Pip's disgust at being caught in such a trap (p. 346). All his financial troubles could have been solved, but Pip knows that he cannot accept Magwitch's money. Herbert becomes his anchor and promises that together they will weather the storm (p. 359).

Pip asks Magwitch (now known as Provis, p. 345) to tell them his story, and when he has finished something akin to compassion has been aroused in Pip (p. 366). Herbert passes him a note revealing that Compeyson was Miss Havisham's 'lover' (pp. 206, 367). At this point (end of ch. 42) Dickens ended an instalment. This build-up of tension illustrates the technique he employed in writing his stories for magazines.

Magwitch's safety becomes a matter of concern but, before Pip makes plans to smuggle him abroad he must see Miss Havisham and Estella. Bentley Drummle becomes important in the plot at this stage. He is staying at the Blue Boar, and talks about dining with 'the lady' (Estella) which infuriates Pip (p. 370).

At Satis House Pip tells Miss Havisham she has succeeded in deluding him, as well as her relations, about his true patron (p. 373). He puts in a good word for Matthew and Herbert at this point, and says she has misjudged Matthew (p. 205) and that he hopes she will help Herbert (p. 375). Robbed of all hope of marrying Estella now, Pip declares his undying love but is stunned when she says she is to marry Drummle. The news opens the floodgates of his heart (pp. 377–8). The last thing he remembers is Estella's 'incredulous wonder' and Miss Havisham's ghastly expression: he walks the twenty-six miles to London to find Wemmick's note warning, 'Don't go home.'

Next day Pip hears from Wemmick that Compeyson is still alive and looking for Magwitch and that Herbert has moved him to a safer hideout. Wemmick advises extreme caution, so Pip secretly visits Magwitch to assure him that they will do all they can to ensure his safety (p. 390). They await a signal from Wemmick. Pip's own character is developing: he now cares for someone other than himself.

Depressed by weeks of waiting for word from Wemmick, Pip goes to the theatre. Compeyson sits behind him, 'like a ghost', and alerts Pip to the constant danger he is in (p. 399). A chance invitation to dine with Jaggers results in Pip's being able to solve some of the Magwitch mystery (p. 403). Wemmick recalls Molly's trial and tells Pip of Jaggers's brilliance in her defence.

A contrite Miss Havisham summons Pip back to Satis House. She authorizes an anonymous payment to Herbert (p. 409), offers money to Pip and implores forgiveness for the great wrong she has done him Pip learns all about Estella before he leaves. He has not gone far before 'a childish association' (p. 94) makes him turn back (p. 414). One minute Miss Havisham is sitting by the fire; the next she is engulfed by flames, screaming and running to him. In his effort to save her, Pip is badly burned.

Herbert provides the last piece of the puzzle in the Magwitch mystery. While he dresses Pip's wound he tells him more about Magwitch and Molly (p. 417f), leaving no doubt that the convict is Estella's father. Pip is able to tell Jaggers something that he does not know (p. 422).

Herbert's friendship sustains Pip through all his troubles and when he finalizes Herbert's financial backing, he knows it is the only decent thing he has ever done. Wemmick names the day for the escape, but Orlick lures Pip into his trap just beforehand. This episode is important for the light it sheds on Pip's reformation (p. 436).

Pip's better nature is most evident during the last stages of the Magwitch story. Compeyson has given Magwitch away and so the daring escape bid fails (p. 454). Pip supports his badly-wounded benefactor with all the devotion of a son. Before Herbert leaves for Cairo, he tells Pip that there will always be a place for him in the firm and his home (p. 460). Magwitch stands trial but dies in prison before the sentence is carried out. His last days are peaceful and he knows human warmth – including the news that Pip loves his daughter – for the first time in his life (p. 470).

Pip is saved from the Debtors' Prison by a fever which makes him ill for weeks. When he regains consciousness he is overjoyed to see dear Joe nursing him back to health (p. 472).

Suddenly Joe disappears but Pip resolves to follow him to the forge to beg forgiveness and to ask Biddy to marry him. He arrives on the day that Joe marries Biddy (p. 487).

But there is some consolation for Pip after all. He meets Estella again eleven years later and they are both the wiser for their experiences. They promise each other friendship as they step out, hand in hand, looking to the future.

# An Account of the Plot

Philip Pirrip, known as Pip, begins his narrative in an isolated and neglected churchyard, close to the river, one Christmas Eve. A forlorn orphan – a 'small bundle of shivers growing afraid of it all' – he is overwhelmed by the desolation and moved to tears when he suddenly realizes that he is alone in the world, his family lying there 'dead and buried'. Even the fact of his father's 'exaltation to a better world' (p. 73) cannot comfort him.

Already frightened, he is truly scared when a hideous man looms up 'from among the graves' without any warning at all and seizes him violently by the chin. Pip is tipped upside-down to empty his pockets, put upon a tombstone and tipped up and down again until he feels giddy and sick. The man is menacing, ruthless, quite without mercy. Pip is forced, under pain of torture and certain death, to promise food and a file, to deliver them the next morning, and to tell no one. No place will be safe if he fails to keep his promise, not even his own bed, as there is a young man about who delights in 'getting at a boy' and at his heart and liver.

Pip watches the convict make for the low church wall. His fear sparks his vivid imagination so that he sees the stranger avoiding the arms of the dead, to prevent himself being pulled underground as he picks his way between the tombs. He begins to run. When he turns to look again the man is limping towards the river, and Pip's wild terror convinces him that the man must be a resurrected pirate going to hook himself back up on the gibbet down by the water's edge. Petrified by his thoughts and the enormity of the dishonest task ahead of him, Pip glances furtively about him for the young man who tears boys apart, then runs home without stopping.

Although Pip begins his narrative with this famous and dramatic scene, it is not the beginning of the story. Much has happened before this moment which Pip could not possibly know about. Nor could he possibly foresee how his life would be entangled in the lives of Magwitch and Miss Havisham. First person narrative is more intimate, but it sometimes causes problems in unravelling a plot. This complex plot leaves many examination students puzzled after the first reading, so do not worry if you feel hazy at this point.

Pip's story is not a straightforward account of how his expectations materialize. Other characters have great expectations, too, and their stories are an integral part of his. In one of these, Miss Havisham plays the lead. That story begins for Pip on p. 82 when he is 'soaped', 'kneaded', 'towelled', 'thumped', 'harrowed', 'rasped', 'put into clean linen' and sent, care of Pumblechook, to play at Miss Havisham's house.

In the other story, Magwitch plays the lead and that drama has just begun for him. Such a frightful experience would haunt any child for life. For Pip it does – in more ways than one.

This chapter is important because it puts Pip in touch with 'the taint of prison and crime' which provides the background to his story, and it is a stratagem that enables the author to develop his 'grotesque tragi-comic conception' of making a convict a gentleman's benefactor.

## CHAPTER 2, *pp. 39–47*

When Pip arrives home, Joe is alone, and Mrs Joe is out looking for him. She returns grumbling about the two of them in general and Pip in particular. As he watches her prepare the tea, it is apparent that Pip's dilemma is how he will save his share for his 'dreadful acquaintance', especially as Joe always keeps an eye on him. As they are fellow-sufferers in Mrs Joe's company, he has devised secret signs to keep Pip's spirits up, one being to compare bites while eating their bread-and-butter. Pip's decision to slip his down his trouser leg has disastrous consequences. Joe thinks he has 'bolted' it in one mouthful and Mrs Joe is quick to notice his astonishment. She bullies an explanation out of him and Pip feels responsible for the violence. They are both dosed with tar-water.

Later that evening, Pip learns that the gun-fire from the marshes signals a second convict's escape. He spends a restless night scared by thoughts of losing his heart and liver, of the convict, and of what he has promised to steal at first light.

Notice Joe's concern for Pip in this chapter (and in chs 3–7, all of which contain vivid portrayals of Pip's childhood) and Joe's sympathetic relationship with him. Dickens's friend, adviser and biographer, John Forster, tells us that this relationship was intended to be 'very funny', and there are some delightful touches of humour in these early chapters.

## CHAPTER 3, *pp. 48–52*

Guilt weighs heavily on Pip as, clutching his stolen 'wittles', he journeys uncomfortably through the mist to keep his fearful appointment. When he mistakes Compeyson, the second escaped convict, for Magwitch, he is sure this must be the young man who tears boys apart and that he is about to breathe his last. But to his relief Compeyson swears at him and escapes into the fog.

He finds Magwitch at the Battery, still in a bad way, limping and hugging himself to keep warm. He eats like a ravenous dog, and Pip watches the food disappear at an amazing rate. He mentions that he could not manage to get any more for the young man. Magwitch is amused at first, until he realizes that Pip has seen Compeyson. He works himself into a frenzy then, determined to get at him; but first he must file off his leg-iron. Pip runs home but the convict is so engrossed in the filing that he does not even notice his going.

The mystery of the other convict is disclosed on p. 366, but he is heard of again later this Christmas Day (and on p. 204).

It takes some courage to set off into the mist with stolen goods to meet an escaped convict, even if you have been terrified by the threat of a bogey-man. Pip's conscience-stricken imagination adds some humour to this graphic scene of mist and dampness.

## CHAPTER 4, *pp. 53–61*

Joe gives Pip a secret sign that Mrs Joe is in a bad mood, even though it is Christmas Day. While she prepares for the visitors, Pip and Joe go to church uncomfortably dressed in their best clothes. The company (p. 55) arrives in time for Christmas dinner and, although Mrs Joe's temper has improved by then, Pip is too preoccupied with his own guilt to appreciate any changes.

The hated grown-ups make Pip's life miserable by their pompous comments implying his ungrateful behaviour in his sister's house. He wishes only to be left alone. The homily about the pig throws light on his position there, and the Victorian attitude to orphans of his class.

Soon, Christmas dinner comes to an end and Pip's 'crime' is about to be discovered; he can hardly control himself. As Mrs Joe fetches the stone bottle containing the adulterated brandy Pip shakes with fear and horrified anticipation. He grips the table-leg to steady himself. When Uncle Pumblechook, having tasted some, rushes out throwing a fit, Pip is certain that murder will be added to his list of offences. He survives that crisis only to face another when it is time to fetch in the pie. He clutches the table-leg again, until he can bear the tension no longer – he rushes to the door and straight into the soldiers standing there holding handcuffs.

What do you think of the obnoxious character Pumblechook? Pip uses some powerful words to describe him both now and later.

## CHAPTER 5, *pp. 61–71*

The soldiers interrupt the dinner-party to ask the blacksmith to repair their broken handcuffs. Two convicts are loose on the marshes and they intend to recapture them at dusk. Joe lights the forge fire, and soon everyone has gathered round to watch. Briefly, they all enjoy a merry Christmas except Pip who, although relieved not to be hand-cuffed, is still troubled on account of his wickedness and the 'poor wretches' outside.

Wopsle, Pip and Joe join the search-party, and after some time they hear shouting. The convicts, Magwitch and Compeyson, are discovered 'struggling at the bottom of a ditch' both of them swearing and bleeding. Pip's convict (Magwitch) boasts that he has captured the other (Compeyson) and seems well pleased, even though it means he has forfeited his own freedom as he had a good chance of getting away without his leg-iron. The other convict accuses Magwitch of trying to murder him, but Magwitch replies that he preferred to keep him alive and hand him over. 'He's a gentleman, if you please, this villain. Now the Hulks has got its gentleman again.' Magwitch is settling an old score.

Pip is anxious to give Magwitch a sign that he has not betrayed him. Their eyes meet. Pip cannot understand his expression but it is a look that he never forgets. Before he is taken by boat to the Hulk, the convict declares that he himself stole the food from the blacksmith's household.

Pip thinks he has seen the last of Magwitch as, by the light of torches, he watches the fugitive being rowed back to the Hulk.

When the soldiers appear at the door at the beginning of this chapter, Pip thinks his last hour has come. By the end, when the convict is taken back to the grim prison-ship having exonerated him, the terror that so quickly possessed him the day before has just as suddenly been lifted. He does not expect to see Magwitch again, but the man has great expectations.

## CHAPTER 6, *pp. 71–3*

Pip knows he should tell Joe the truth, especially about his missing file, but he cannot risk spoiling their relationship. He loves Joe too much and cannot bear the thought of his disapproval. As he observes, 'I was too cowardly to do what I knew to be right, as I had been too cowardly to avoid doing what I knew to be wrong.'

Joe carries Pip home after the convicts have been caught. When they get back, Pumblechook pontificates on the convict's method of entry, and everyone agrees with him because they feel they have to.

## CHAPTER 7, *pp. 73–83*

About a year later Pip is an odd-boy about the forge (not being old enough yet to be apprenticed to Joe) and to any neighbours who need an extra pair of hands. He attends the Dame-school run by Mr Wopsle's eccentric old great-aunt. She regularly falls asleep, to the amusement of the students. Her granddaughter, Biddy, works in the general store which is housed in the same room.

Pip struggles with his schooling and eventually manages to write an illiterate letter to Joe while they are both sitting in the kitchen. Joe cannot read it and confesses his lack of education. He tells Pip about his childhood, and of the early days when he first met Pip's sister, who was bringing Pip up 'by hand'. When he eventually proposed to her, Joe invited her to 'bring the poor little child' to live with them at the forge. Pip is overcome with emotion and flings his arms round Joe.

They secretly agree to educate Joe, because Mrs Joe would feel inferior if she knew she had two scholars in the house! Joe likes her to have her own way and does not really mind that she is 'given to government'. His mother had had such a dreadful time as a drudge, that Joe is determined that Mrs Joe shall not suffer in the same way. The relationship between Joe and Pip is strengthened as a result of Joe's confidences and Pip admires and respects him.

Mrs Joe has been to market with Pumblechook, and they return with news that is to turn Pip's life upside-down. He is to stay that night with Pumblechook, who will, the next morning, take him to Miss Havisham's to play. Mrs Joe suggests that his fortune may be made if he goes there; Pip knows, as does everyone else, that Miss Havisham is 'an immensely rich and grim lady who [lives] in a large and dismal house, barricaded against robbers, and who [leads] a life of seclusion'.

This chapter marks the end of Pip's contentment, but all that he has learnt from Joe – by the kitchen fireside, and in the forge – will never desert him. Time and again in the future he will look back nostalgically to these days.

Just in case you cannot decipher Pip's letter (see p. 75), it reads as follows:

My dear Joe,
I hope you are quite well. I hope I shall soon be able for to teach you Joe, and then we shall all be so glad, and when I'm apprenticed to you, Joe, what larks and believe me,

in affection
Pip.

## CHAPTER 8, *pp. 83–94*

Pip's time with Pumblechook is miserable, consisting of diluted rations for breakfast and endless mental arithmetic tests. He is glad to leave him in the morning at the iron gate of Satis House and to follow Estella into the dark mansion.

From the start she is condescending, but Pip cannot help being fascinated by her beauty and self-possession. She leaves him outside Miss Havisham's door so Pip knocks and goes in.

He stands just inside the strange room and looks at the even stranger lady. The candlelit room is large and airless; if there are windows they have been screened to black out the sun and shut out fresh air. Pip is overwhelmed by the eerie atmosphere.

Dominating the room is the melancholy Miss Havisham, dressed in her faded bridal-gown, sitting at a 'fine lady's dressing-table' and surrounded by the abandoned paraphernalia of a society wedding. She has a strange look upon her face, and Pip is afraid.

She calls him across to her and tells him her heart has been broken. Pip is so dumbfounded that he cannot play when she tells him to. Estella is summoned to play cards, despite her reluctance to play with such a 'common labouring-boy'. Pip thinks he hears Miss Havisham say, 'well, you can break his heart'.

They sit down to play and Pip takes in more details of both the extraordinary room and the even more extraordinary Miss Havisham. Estella wins the games and misses no opportunity to make Pip feel uncomfortable.

For the first time Pip is ashamed of his background and in the yard, where Estella feeds him like a dog, he wishes he had not been brought up to call the knaves Jacks. He is so deeply hurt that he is driven to tears and acts of frustration. When he regains control of himself, he explores the grounds, but sees Estella at every turn (and forever after – see p. 378). A vision of Miss Havisham hanging from a beam frightens him, but he recovers his senses just as Estella comes to unlock the gate. She mocks him again, and he goes on his way deploring his lack of breeding.

Until he met Estella, Pip had been content to be himself – but not any more. Looking at his 'coarse hands' and 'thick boots' he says (pp. 91–2):

They had never troubled me before, but they troubled me now, as vulgar appendages . . . I wished Joe had been rather more genteelly brought up, and then I should have been so, too.

This chapter is important because it introduces Pip to artificial values, to snobbery, and it is the starting point for all his dissatisfaction and for his misconceptions about wealth and gentility.

**CHAPTER 9,** *pp. 95–101*

Pip plays to the gallery as he relates his 'pretended experiences' to his sister and Pumblechook, delighting in every moment of the deception. But when Mrs Joe tells Joe, Pip's feelings change. He cannot deceive Joe. He goes to the forge later and confesses the lies that he is unable to account for, but he tries to explain how he feels about being common, and how impressed he is by the 'beautiful young lady . . . who was dreadfully proud'. Joe tells him that in his experience it is more comfortable to mix with people of his own class in familiar surroundings and, whatever the reason, there is never an excuse for lies. He encourages Pip to 'live well and die happy'. In bed that night Pip feels ashamed again – this time of Joe and 'of sitting in the kitchen'.

## CHAPTER 10, *pp. 101–8*

Biddy agrees to give Pip private lessons so that he can 'get on in life', and after one such lesson Pip calls for Joe at the Three Jolly Bargemen on his way home. He finds Joe with Wopsle and a stranger who watches Pip as he talks with the other two. The stranger buys the men rum and, when they look away, stirs his own drink with Joe's stolen file, still looking at Pip all the while.

As they leave, the stranger gives Pip a shilling wrapped up in two one-pound notes. Joe walks home with his mouth wide open to get rid of the smell of the rum. Pip is haunted by thoughts of the convict. When the pound notes are discovered by Mrs Joe, Joe runs back to return them; Pip knows the stranger will have gone. The notes are put in the parlour and serve as a permanent reminder of his 'conspiracy with convicts'.

Dickens is famous for his brief pen-portraits and he brings the stranger to life in a few words. He is likened to a man holding an invisible gun and taking aim. Once you realize this, you can understand the later references. For example, 'aiming eye' (p. 107) is a brilliantly suggestive choice of words, so much more colourful than describing the man's physical limitations literally. In a few masterly strokes, Dickens does this again and again, as one character after another is clearly created.

The 'taint of prison and crime' is never far from Pip. His nightmares return and he is petrified again after seeing the file.

## CHAPTER 11, *pp. 108–21*

On his second visit to Satis House, Pip waits in another room. There he comes upon Miss Havisham's relations criticizing one Matthew and making mountains out of molehills. He senses their insincerity.

A bell rings and Estella takes Pip upstairs, tormenting him so spitefully on the way that he vows never to cry over her again. They meet Jaggers coming down. (Pip does not yet know who he is.)

Pip is sent to the room opposite where there are further signs of Miss Havisham's blighted hopes in the crumbled remains of happier days. Spiders and mice are the only signs of life.

Pip is obliged to walk Miss Havisham round and round the large table while her relations pay their hypocritical respects on her birthday. When they have gone, the familiar pattern of the visits is resumed, but with one exception.

In the garden, Pip meets 'the pale young gentleman' who challenges him to a fight. Pip is surprised to win and he is impressed by his opponent's behaviour. With a 'bright flush upon her face', Estella allows Pip to kiss her as he leaves.

Notice that Pip admits his vow, never to cry over Estella again, proves to be 'as false a declaration as ever was made'. False it is (see pp. 377–8) but he makes other false vows too, especially concerning Joe, which are much worse.

Note the masterly pen-portrait of another character, Sarah Pocket (p. 115).

## CHAPTER 12, *pp. 121–6*

Each day Pip expects to be punished for his treatment of the 'pale young gentleman', but nothing happens. From now, and on alternate days, Pip has to push Miss Havisham in a garden-chair through the upstairs rooms. This goes on for about ten months during which time, in answer to her questions, Pip tells her that he hopes to be apprenticed to Joe and to improve his own education too.

He sees Estella regularly, but he is never again invited to kiss her. Miss Havisham adds fuel to his fire by drawing attention to her good looks, and sometimes he hears her whisper to Estella, 'break their hearts . . .' (p. 123). The blacksmiths' chorus takes her fancy and, on occasions, all three of them sing it as Pip pushes Miss Havisham around the room in her chair.

Biddy is always available and he confides in her as a matter of course, but he is unaware of her feelings for him. Pumblechook, Pip's self-appointed benefactor, continues to humiliate him in a ridiculous manner. He discusses the boy's prospects with Mrs Joe, who is growing impatient as Pip is old enough to be apprenticed.

Miss Havisham invites Joe, through Pip, to visit and take Pip's indentures. Mrs Joe is so disappointed after all their speculation that she suffers severe emotional shock and 'goes on the Rampage' (p. 126). Mrs Joe is jealous because she had not been invited to Satis House, too, and in her rage forces Joe and Pip outside into the cold while she cleans the house in a more alarming manner than usual. It is past ten o'clock before they dare creep back inside; even then Mrs Joe is still fuming.

For the second time Pip hears 'break their hearts' whispered to Estella. Miss Havisham exploits her ruthlessly. Her great expectation is revenge on all men. What she is actually doing to Estella does not enter her obsessed mind.

Now that Joe has been summoned to see Miss Havisham, who subsequently pays for Pip's apprenticeship, Pip wrongly assumes that she will make his fortune, as his sister and Pumblechook have forecast.

# CHAPTER 13, *pp. 127–34*

Dressed in his best clothes, Joe is at a disadvantage even before he meets Miss Havisham. Once at Satis House he is shocked into silence by the strangeness of the recluse and her surroundings with the result that he can only mumble his replies to Pip whenever Miss Havisham addresses him.

Estella enjoys the spectacle of Joe's embarrassment; Pip feels nothing but shame. Once Miss Havisham has paid the fee for Pip's apprenticeship and warned Joe that that is all they can expect, Estella shows them out and Pip's days at Satis House are apparently over.

Years of living with Mrs Joe have taught Joe how to handle her. He relays to her an invented message from Miss Havisham, which makes her laugh – a rare occurrence – and then hands over the money. Not to be outdone, Pumblechook decides Pip should be bound (see Glossary), and to that end takes him to the Town Hall and later behaves in every way as his benefactor.

Mrs Joe is so excited by the windfall that she wants a family party at the Blue Boar. Since such gatherings of insensitive adults have always been a blot on his cheerless childhood, Pip is in no mood to celebrate approaching manhood in this way.

Pip is now fourteen and at an impressionable age. He has a lot to learn about values and the true worth of people such as Joe and Biddy.

## CHAPTER 14, *pp. 134–6*

Pip reviews the change that has come over him since Estella first made him aware of his 'vulgar appendages'. Joe has been his idol and Joe's influence still prevents him from being any worse. At least he perseveres with his apprenticeship.

Estella is continually on his mind, and his greatest fear is that she should see him at his common work.

Pip has no idea what he is chasing. His dreams of gentility are illusions beyond his understanding and always just below the surface his conscience reminds him of reality.

## CHAPTER 15, *pp. 136–47*

On Sundays Pip and Joe often go to the Battery where Pip tries to 'improve' Joe, but he makes no progress at all. One Sunday Joe agrees to give Pip a half-day to go to Satis House, stipulating that there should be but one visit, unless there is an invitation to return.

Orlick, the journeyman (workman), not to be outdone, insists on a free afternoon, too. Mrs Joe overhears and rebukes her husband for giving 'idle hulkers like that' time off. Orlick showers her with abuse and Mrs Joe screams hysterically, working herself into a frenzy until Joe is forced to take action. When Orlick picks himself up from the coal-dust, Mrs Joe has gone to lie down and peace returns to the forge.

Pip's call is a fruitless one. Estella is abroad preparing to be a lady and Miss Havisham is delighted to give him this news. She says Pip may visit her annually.

Meeting Wopsle in the High Street does nothing to raise Pip's spirits. He is obliged to accompany him to Pumblechook's and take part in the play *George Barnwell* (see p. 502). He resents Pumblechook's insinuation that he can learn something from it.

Orlick joins them as they walk home late. A commotion in the inn alerts them to trouble. There is greater confusion in Pip's kitchen where Mrs Joe is found lying senseless in the middle of the room.

Joe is unaffected by Pip's effort to 'improve' him and content to accept himself as he is. His is the wisdom, and it shines through the novel.

## CHAPTER 16, *pp. 147–51*

Although two convicts escaped from the Hulks the previous night, they are not suspected of the crime against Mrs Joe. The leg-iron by Mrs Joe's unconscious body has been filed too long ago. Pip knows who it belongs to and he is worried that he has had a hand in providing the weapon. He is on the point of telling Joe, but decides not to risk causing a rift in their relationship unless it becomes absolutely crucial in solving the case.

The Bow Street runners are unsuccessful in bringing anyone to justice. Pip's sister has become a pitiable invalid who needs permanent nursing, and as Biddy is free of family ties by then, she becomes housekeeper at the forge. No one can understand Mrs Joe's odd request to see Orlick.

Dickens mocks the Bow Street runners (for whom he had little time) by making them suspect the last person on earth to have committed the crime – Joe.

The mystery about Mrs Joe's strange fascination for Orlick is hard to explain. Perhaps she was sorry that Joe had knocked him down – she fainted at the time. Having been beaten up herself later, perhaps she feels guilty about him. I think she did not know he had attacked her because Orlick said (much later, p. 437): 'I come upon her from behind.' The leg-iron is another reminder for Pip of his frightening experience on the marshes.

## CHAPTER 17, *pp. 152–60*

Satis House has proved to be a bad influence on Pip by blinding him to better people around him. Biddy has grown more attractive and is 'pleasant and wholesome and sweet-tempered', but she is common and that will not do for Pip.

The fact that she is better than he deserves escapes him and he pays no attention to her when she wisely expresses opinions that his conscience has already told him are true (p. 156) about his reason for wanting so much to be a gentleman. Nor does he pay attention to her feelings – 'don't mind me', she says – and he doesn't. Instinctively she knows how to comfort him and she is glad of his confidence, but the relationship goes no further than that.

On the way home from the marshes they come upon Orlick, slouching as usual, and he is all for inflicting his unpleasant company upon them. In response to Biddy's whispered plea, Pip gives Orlick short shrift and later protects Biddy from him in the forge. Orlick hates Pip and bears him a grudge for years (p. 435).

In his heart of hearts, Pip knows that 'all that Biddy said seemed right' (p. 157); he knows 'the plain honest working life to which I was born, had nothing in it to be ashamed of' (p. 159). He knows his roots are with 'dear old Joe and the forge' and a life with Biddy would be a happy one. But he believes in fairy-stories and expects Miss Havisham to make his fortune.

**CHAPTER 18,** *pp. 160–72*

One Saturday night when Pip is eighteen, Wopsle entertains the villagers in the Jolly Bargemen with a dramatic account of a murder reported in the paper. He pronounces the accused man guilty, whereupon a stranger (Jaggers) cross-questions him until he is made to look ridiculous.

Pip recognizes the stranger as the gentleman with the scented hands whom he had met at Satis House (p. 111). He has come with private news for Joe and Pip. The conference is held in the state parlour of the forge. Jaggers announces that he is acting confidentially on behalf of his client and that Pip has great expectations. There are certain conditions (p. 165) to which he may object if he does so at once: Pip has no objections to the conditions.

Jaggers, now his guardian, gives him money, instructing him to buy new clothes and to be ready to leave for London the following week to begin his education and to become a gentleman.

Jaggers gets more than he bargains for when he offers Joe compensation for the loss of his apprentice. Money is Jaggers's lifeblood, so he is amazed by the blacksmith's refusal and even more amazed to find himself backing away from an angry man!

Jaggers returns to London leaving an uncomfortable silence in the kitchen; but Joe tells Biddy the news and they both congratulate Pip. They talk about who Pip should show his clothes to and where and when; it is all rather hollow and Pip is surprised by his doubts and uneasy sleep.

Jaggers is the first link with Miss Havisham, Matthew (p. 166) the second. Pip is sure now that she will make his fortune.

**CHAPTER 19,** *pp. 173–86*

By next morning Pip is dreaming of fame and fortune as he takes a last walk across the marshes after lunch. Joe follows him to the Battery and Pip promises 'dear Joe ... I shall never forget you'

(p. 174). He explains: 'I had always wanted to be a gentleman', and this notion astonishes Joe. It is something he cannot understand.

Pip worries about Joe's ignorance, and discusses with Biddy the need to change him. Believing himself to be set apart and different in some inexplicable way from ordinary folk, Pip assumes airs and graces that hurt Biddy, although she manages to control her feelings.

With quiet confidence and a touch of calm sarcasm, she puts Pip in his place and, at the same time, applauds Joe's natural, well-respected place in the village. She points out his dignity and pride, and reminds Pip that both Joe and Pip know that he would be out of place in higher society. If these are faults, so what? There is nothing wrong with Joe's manners or his background.

Pip resents Biddy's tone. He accuses her of envy and says that criticizing someone else is a 'bad side of human nature' (pp. 176, 302).

He goes into town the next day where he experiences 'the stupendous power of money'. Those who have it could expect to be worshipped, and Trabb and Pumblechook certainly reverence his 'sacred person' (p. 179 f).

In his gentleman's clothes, he says goodbye to Miss Havisham on the eve of his departure. Still starry-eyed, he imagines her stick to be his fairy godmother's wand adding the finishing touches before he sets out on his adventure (p. 183). That she has heard about his fortune only serves to convince him that she initiated it. He takes his leave of her with a flourish – in the best tradition of the melodrama.

During his last evening with Biddy and Joe, Pip leaves a number of things unsaid. Once out of sight of 'dear old Joe' waving and Biddy wiping a tear on her apron – and before he steps out into the unknown – Pip sheds tears, too, which soften him and almost make him turn back (p. 186).

Pip, although dressed as a gentleman, has not the least idea what it means to be one. His ideas are shallow and he believes that money, fine clothes and education are all he needs. It will be a long time before he learns that these are false attributes, and that wealth and gentility are not equivalents.

This chapter is important because, unaware of the sacrifices he is about to make and heedless of the voices of wisdom and common sense (Joe's and Biddy's), Pip sets out into the great unknown with nothing to hold on to except a subconscious belief in fairy-stories. Thus ends the first stage of Pip's expectations.

## CHAPTER 20, *pp. 187–94*

Pip alights from the coach into another world, and his first feeling about London is that it is dirty and dismal. Jaggers's office only adds to this impression. Amid the clutter of neglected legal trappings, two dusty casts (p. 188) dominate the dark room, and Pip decides to wait for Jaggers (who is in Court) outside.

He has his first ugly sight of Smithfield followed by a brief introduction to Newgate which 'was horrible and gave me a sickening idea of London'. Others are waiting for Jaggers, too, and it is quite obvious from their conversations that they hold him in high esteem and hope to enlist his support. As Jaggers approaches these clients flock to him and, while he walks back to the office with Pip, he dismisses them, one by one, with encouragement, a threat or a scathing comment.

Jaggers is not above calling in false witnesses (p. 193) provided his name is not directly involved. 'The stupendous power of money' is the driving force behind the lawyer, and this is illustrated by the speed with which he dispatches Pip to Barnard's Inn, accompanied by Wemmick, while he takes lunch standing up.

So much for Pip's idea of London: the illusory and the real are often poles apart. He cannot escape the 'taint of prison and crime'.

## CHAPTER 21, *pp. 195–9*

On the short walk to Barnard's Inn, Pip studies Wemmick, but he does not immediately warm to him. As they approach the chambers Pip is dismayed to see 'a collection of shabby buildings', not at all what he had expected, and while he waits alone for Mr Pocket Junior, upon whose door is a notice 'Return shortly', Pip is further disappointed by the filthy surroundings.

The young gentleman arrives about half-an-hour later, bearing tokens of hospitality, and extends a breathless welcome as he wrestles with the front door. Once over the threshold, they stare at each other in amazement: for they have met before at Satis House (p. 118).

Here is another link with Miss Havisham which gives Pip more 'evidence' about his 'benefactress'.

## CHAPTER 22, *pp. 199–211*

Distance certainly lends enchantment to Herbert's view of their fight, but Pip does not contradict him. He is more interested in what Herbert has to tell him about Estella and Miss Havisham, and why she should want to 'wreak revenge on all the male sex'. But he has to wait until dinner-time.

Meanwhile, Pip explains how he came to be at Satis House that day, but when Herbert mentions Miss Havisham and Jaggers in the same breath, mindful of his donor's instructions, he discourages his companion from jumping to any conclusion (p. 201), saying he has not seen Jaggers since.

Pip is attracted by Herbert's 'frank and easy way'. His personality expresses 'a natural incapacity to do anything secret and mean', and they enjoy a friendly relationship on Christian name terms from the start, although Herbert chooses to change Pip's name to Handel. (Pip has reason to be particularly glad of that later, p. 250.)

During the meal, Herbert tells Pip all he knows about Miss Havisham, interrupting his narrative only to mention, in the kindest possible way, how people in polite society behave.

Because Herbert's father had tried to warn Miss Havisham of Compeyson's (his name is not mentioned in ch. 22) untrustworthiness, she had ordered him out of her house. Pip asks Herbert if Matthew feels bitter towards her. Herbert says it is not that, but Miss Havisham had accused him (in front of Compeyson) of trying to take advantage of her, and that accusation had prevented him from visiting her ever since because 'it would look true'.

Herbert finishes his story on a vague note, saying that the two men (Compeyson and Arthur) went from bad to worse; but he does not know if they are still alive. Neither does he know when Estella was adopted by Miss Havisham.

Herbert has great expectations of being successful in the City, but he is still getting his bearings. Pip has the impression that he will never be very prosperous and as it soon transpires that Herbert has not even started earning money yet, he seems to be right.

By the end of the weekend Pip 'had put the poor old kitchen at home far away' and on Monday Herbert takes him to Hammersmith to meet his family.

Dickens discloses the reason for Miss Havisham's eccentric self-imprisonment, but no names have yet been mentioned. Compeyson is part of the Magwitch mystery, but at this stage Pip has no reason to connect him with his convict – or to realize that he has actually seen him. We begin to wonder about Estella's parentage.

This chapter is important because the three stories intersect. It is important, too, because we see an example of true gentility. Herbert has a natural appeal and illustrates his father's definition of a true gentleman (p. 204).

## CHAPTER 23, *pp. 211–19*

This chapter is a charming interlude; it adds little to the development of the story, but contributes plenty to its themes.

Pip meets his tutor and fellow-students. One, Startop, will later come to his rescue (p. 428); the other, Drummle, will plague him at various stages and finally marry his beloved Estella (p. 377).

The cameo portrayed so graphically illustrates the folly of pretending to be something we are not, and the effect such false behaviour has on our own lives as well as other people's.

Study Belinda Pocket's grand ideas that never materialize. Look at the useless life she leads and consider how much her life is a parody of Pip's.

## CHAPTER 24, *pp. 219–25*

Matthew establishes a good relationship with Pip, and brings out the best in him. He gives him sound advice. Once Pip has decided to keep a room at Barnard's Inn, he needs money to furnish it.

Pip has no difficulty in obtaining money from Jaggers, but he has to endure rapid cross-questioning before a figure is agreed and, almost before he knows where he is, he has been passed over to Wemmick who has been instructed to pay him twenty pounds.

While Pip gets his breath back, Wemmick explains that Jaggers's manner is part of his professionalism. He can afford to act as he likes because he has such a good reputation. Wemmick takes Pip on a tour of the offices and back to Jaggers's room where he discovers the horrible truth about the hideous casts (p. 223), and about Wemmick's jewellery and his passion for 'portable property'. He invites Pip to spend a night at his home at some time and adds that when Jaggers invites him to dine, as no doubt he will, Pip should notice the housekeeper – 'a wild beast tamed' (see p. 404). Before they part, Wemmick takes him to see Jaggers in action in court. He is the centre of attraction and authority.

Jaggers's office reflects the bleak picture of crime, prisons and the law that is to hound Pip throughout his quest.

## CHAPTER 25, *pp. 225–32*

Pip soon settles into a routine and works hard at his education. Herbert becomes his closest friend and Startop and Drummle his associates when they go boating.

One day, the other Pockets (first seen at Satis House) visit Hammersmith and Pip has no reason to alter his first impressions – that they are all 'toadies and humbugs' (pp. 109, 226).

Several weeks have passed since Wemmick's invitation, so Pip arranges a date to go to his house. As they walk to Walworth, Pip hears more about the power of Jaggers and his curious hold over people.

The 'little wooden cottage' that is Wemmick's home and castle has been fashioned to his whimsical taste. He has worked at it little by little and made it a home he is proud of. Aged Parent delights in his son's achievement, and Pip is pleased to keep nodding to delight the old man. He nods himself silly when the gun fires, a nightly ceremony devised to give Aged Parent a treat, but still the old man would have more.

The Walworth Wemmick is not the mechanical clerk Pip first met on coming to London. Pip is intrigued by the way he becomes an altogether different person in private life. This is not the Wemmick that Jaggers knows. Pip thoroughly enjoys his visit.

Next morning they walk back to Little Britain, and the nearer they get the more automatic and official Wemmick becomes.

John Wemmick is not the only one who adopts different roles for office and home but it is extraordinary that he is able to separate the two so completely.

## CHAPTER 26, *pp. 232–9*

As expected, Jaggers invites Pip and the other gentlemen to dine at his large home where everything is functional rather than decorative. Jaggers is drawn to Drummle as a kindred spirit. They are both bullies. Remembering Wemmick's advice, Pip takes a long look at the housekeeper, Molly, who reminds him of one of Macbeth's apparitions, and he notes how she seems afraid of displeasing Jaggers.

During the meal Jaggers applies the psychology that dispels inhibitions, and before he is aware of it, Pip is boasting of his extravagance and prospects; Drummle has lost his party manners if ever he had any! The evening proceeds gaily (p. 235), voices are raised and arms bared, and in this commotion Jaggers traps Molly's hand as she stretches across the table.

He draws everyone's attention to the strength of her wrists; she is clearly uneasy and glad to escape when Jaggers gives her a sign. Before long the party is in uproar again, but before Drummle can throw his glass at Startop, Jaggers seizes it and announces that the evening is at an end.

Pip returns briefly to apologize but Jaggers makes light of it all, adding that although he likes Spider (Drummle) Pip should steer clear of him.

## CHAPTER 27, *pp. 239–47*

Biddy's letter to say that Joe is coming to London is not welcome, and Pip can raise no enthusiasm for Joe's visit. He is rich, reckless and idle but the one thing his money cannot do is keep Joe away (p. 240).

Anxious not to offend Pip, Joe is anything but relaxed and the two speak as strangers, each feeling embarrassment for different reasons. Joe manages to give some news about the people at home, including Wopsle, who has great expectations of playing Hamlet at a small London theatre.

Herbert joins them for breakfast – a fraught affair – and when he has gone to work, Pip is relieved. He is unaware that he is responsible for Joe's discomfort. They have grown so far apart, but it is not Joe who has changed. Pip is conscious of the qualities that Biddy had mentioned so long ago (p. 175): 'I was conscious of a sort of dignity in the look' (p. 245).

When Joe tells Pip the real reason for his visit (p. 246) – that Estella wants to see him – Pip at least has the grace to blush. As he leaves, Joe takes the blame for the failure of their meeting, saying that he feels out of place, and that Pip would not find so much to criticize if they were to meet in his own surroundings. He takes his leave 'with simple dignity' that brings tears to Pip's eyes and stirs his conscience.

This chapter (and ch. 26) is important because Pip is at his lowest ebb in all things false (and he stays that way, on the whole, until his long walk home, p. 378). Corrupted by position and wealth, he sets himself upon a pedestal and looks down on Joe.

## CHAPTER 28, *pp. 247–53*

Likening himself to a counterfeit coin being passed as genuine, Pip acknowledges his falseness in deciding to stay at the Blue Boar instead of at Joe's, when he goes to see Miss Havisham and Estella the next day.

By chance, two convicts are travelling on the coach with him, and by an even greater chance, one of them is the stranger that Pip had last seen in the Jolly Bargemen (p. 103). Pip has never been more grateful for the nickname – Handel – with which Herbert bids him farewell.

During the long journey, Pip dozes off. It is dark when he awakes, and from the darkness one of the convicts' voices is heard unfolding the events that led up to an incident involving 'two one-pound notes'. Images of Magwitch, remembrances of his childhood terror, and fear of being recognized prompt Pip to leave the coach on the outskirts of town and walk the rest of the journey.

He follows the two convicts, in his vivid imagination, over the same ground that Magwitch covered back to the prison-ship all those years ago. He is uneasy and alarmed by the memory of it.

At the Blue Boar, Pip reads a report in the local paper about his 'rise to fortune', for which Pumblechook takes the credit for being his 'earliest patron and the founder of his fortunes'.

The 'taint of prison' is still around, like mists that will not clear, especially when Estella is in Pip's thoughts. In his excitement about her he soon forgets Joe. So much for his promise (p. 174)!

## CHAPTER 29, *pp. 253–65*

With high hopes Pip goes to Satis House early next morning. He feels certain that Miss Havisham intends Estella for him, but is shocked to find Orlick on duty with a loaded gun, and he mentions this to Jaggers later (p. 265).

Estella is even more beautiful that day, and it takes Pip a moment or two to recognize her. Her power is as compelling as before and he knows, without a doubt, that she is an inseparable part of his innermost life. They recall old times as they walk round the garden, but Pip still feels inferior to her. He believes he is 'set apart for her' and cannot accept her admission that she has no heart. She reminds him of someone, but he is not quick enough to grasp the vague likenesses (p. 259).

While Estella dresses for dinner, Pip has an extraordinary time with Miss Havisham. She lapses into a melodramatic mood, telling him to love Estella come what may, and gives him a definition of love not too far removed from the thoughts he has been having (see pp. 253–4).

Jaggers appears and he and Pip join Estella and Sarah Pocket for dinner. He reveals nothing when Pip asks about Estella's name. During dinner he enjoys tormenting Sarah Pocket by referring to Pip's expectations (she is very jealous) and she does not join them afterwards for cards.

Back at the Blue Boar Pip can think of nothing but Estella's dazzling beauty.

There are references here to their childhood days which you might be able to place. If not, see p. 121 for the reward Pip recalls on p. 258.

It is now two days since Joe's visit to London when Pip had feelings of remorse. Pip is under the spell of 'the dreamy room . . . the old strange influences . . .' and Estella has said 'what was fit company for you once, would be quite unfit company for you now'. He does not give Joe another thought.

## CHAPTER 30, *pp. 265–73*

Pip has arranged to meet Jaggers on the midday coach. Before that Jaggers will return to Satis House to sack Orlick, and Pip will make a detour of the town to avoid Pumblechook. Little does Pip know what mortification is in store for him.

At first he relishes the attention his 'sacred person' (p. 179) is attracting again as he struts along the street, every inch a gentleman. Then the pantomime begins. Trabb's boy makes such a fool of Pip with his intelligent mime and mimicry that the gathering onlookers shout for joy. Pip is powerless; all he can do is to complain in writing to Trabb.

Once in London, he eases his conscience regarding Joe by sending an expensive gift. He tells Herbert all that happened at Satis House. Herbert confesses his secret engagement to Clara. Later they go to see Wopsle's play to cheer themselves up.

Trabb's boy is a shrewd lad not to be taken in by a sham. Pip has to learn that he must win respect; he cannot buy it.

Herbert reads Pip like a book and he knows of his adoration for Estella even before the confidence is imparted. He knows, too, that the relationship cannot succeed as it is unnatural and based on false values. His advice to Pip is to give her up. Suddenly Pip feels as he did on leaving the forge (pp. 186, 271). He knows Herbert is right, but he is bewitched by Estella.

## CHAPTER 31, *pp. 273–9*

Shakespeare's tragedy is unrecognizable in Wopsle's (Waldengarver's) hands. It is nothing but a farce from beginning to end; the audience participates by jeering, commenting rudely and even throwing nuts.

In his dressing-room Wopsle tells Pip and Herbert that he has given an intelligent performance before an unreceptive audience and that things can only improve in time. He dines at Barnard's Inn with them and stays until two o'clock in the morning talking about his success and his great expectation of reviving the drama.

The play does nothing to cheer Pip up, and he has a nightmare, 'that my expectations were all cancelled' (p. 279).

There is an obvious analogy between Wopsle's illusions and Pip's. Each pretends to be someone he is not; each deludes himself by 'reviewing his success and developing his plans'. As these expectations are built on false values neither can hope to succeed. No wonder Pip has a nightmare; or is it a prophetic dream?

Dickens's reference to *Hamlet* (Wopsle's play) is relevant to Pip's own story; '. . . to thine own self be true' will prove to be sound advice.

## CHAPTER 32, *pp. 279–84*

As previously arranged (p. 264) Estella sends a note to Pip, telling him of her time of arrival in London. That same day Wemmick has business with a client at Newgate and on his way there meets Pip waiting at the coach-office. As he has four or five hours to spare, Pip goes with Wemmick to Newgate; he later wishes he had not.

Prison neglect and degradation form the normal background to Wemmick's work, so it does not affect him. He moves carefully among the prisoners, recognizing each one, and, although many ask him questions they dare not ask Jaggers they know where to draw the line. Sending Wemmick is all part of Jaggers's way of doing business. He stays aloof but gets all the information he needs.

In the three hours still to wait after his visit to Newgate, Pip cannot clear his mind of the 'taint of prison and crime' (p. 284). It seems to have been a part of his life ever since he met the convict on the marshes. Utterly disgusted, he beats, shakes and exhales the contamination of prison out of his system.

As Estella approaches once again he wonders of whom she reminds him.

The last time Pip saw Estella he had travelled with convicts. This time he has just visited convicts. Always he is haunted by convicts. He reflects on 'the contrast between the jail and her' as though there could not be any link. This is ironic.

## CHAPTER 33, *pp. 284–91*

Estella is even more beautiful than before. She tells Pip of their instructions, explaining that they are not free to please themselves. In a private room of the coaching-inn, she talks about the influential, well-connected lady in Richmond, who will introduce her into society. She condemns the wily Pocket family, all but Matthew, and Pip sees her laugh for the first time at the idea of the Pockets getting anywhere with Miss Havisham. She assures him that whatever poison they spread it will make no difference to Miss Havisham's plans; she offers her hand on that which Pip kisses. When he kisses her on the cheek she reminds him of their instructions. He rings for tea, pays the bill, tips everyone liberally and they set off for Richmond in the coach.

Passing Newgate, Pip is conscious again of the strange feeling that he had before (p. 289). It interrupts their conversation so that he omits to tell Estella about the time he dined with Jaggers (see pp. 235, 403). The rest of the journey is uneventful but for the memorable moment when she speaks his name for the first time. He knows it is a psychological ploy to enchant him, but he is powerless under her spell. Having delivered his charge safely, Pip returns to Hammersmith with heavy heart.

It is, of course, Estella's likeness to Molly, Jaggers's housekeeper, that gives Pip his 'inexplicable feeling' – and the 'taint of prison and crime' in the background adds to the mystery. In spite of all the warnings, Pip is convinced that Miss Havisham has their future under control.

## CHAPTER 34, *pp. 291–9*

With no clear purpose to his life, Pip drifts into lazy and extravagant ways, taking Herbert with him. He often recalls the comfort and warmth of his innocent, childhood days and wonders how different he would have been without expectations.

As it is he indulges himself in every foolish pleasure that money can buy. The Finches of the Grove typifies the falseness of his life: this is an exclusive London club for the idle rich, and Pip and Herbert put their names down for membership. The strength of their friend-ship is tested as they plunge deeper and deeper into debt, and grow more and more disheartened; but they see each other through it. When the mood takes them, they lull themselves into a state of false security by looking into their affairs and leaving a margin (pp. 295–6)!

On one such occasion, Pip receives news from Trabb and Co. that his sister has died.

## CHAPTER 35, *pp. 297–304*

Mrs Joe's funeral is an outward show to impress the neighbours. Trabb and Co. organize the elaborate proceedings; villagers come to watch. Draped in black trappings, the mourners follow the hearse behind Pip and Joe, their pocket handkerchiefs at the ready, and process through the village to the churchyard. Before and after the ceremony, Pumblechook stuffs himself with sherry and biscuits, as insensitive as usual to those about him.

When all the mourners have gone, Joe changes into comfortable clothes. This is the first time Biddy has seen Pip since he left home, and her 'downcast eyes' (pp. 301–2) reflect the hurt she still feels. She has not forgotten what he said about the 'bad side of human nature' (pp. 176, 302) either.

She brings him up to date with events: since she can no longer remain at Joe's house she hopes to teach at the new school; Mrs Joe died with her arms round Joe's neck and the words 'Joe', 'pardon' and 'Pip' on her lips; Orlick continues to be a nuisance. Pip hardens against him (pp. 303, 435).

She speaks in glowing terms of Joe and all that he stands for, and of Joe's love for Pip. Biddy knows Pip better than he knows himself, and she greets his intention to 'be often down' with stony silence. When pressed she replies, 'Are you quite sure, then, that you WILL...?'

Once again she has touched his weak spot and he blames *her* 'bad side of human nature', but by the time he leaves next day he knows she is right. He will not be back.

Pip cannot face the truth about himself, so he takes it out on Biddy. It is not unusual for someone who feels inadequate to behave like Pip. He is afraid to admit his inferiority, and this fear motivates his unkindness. Pip finds compensation for his feelings in finding fault in Biddy.

## CHAPTER 36, *pp. 304–11*

On his twenty-first birthday Pip is summoned to Jaggers's office where he is questioned about his rate of expenditure. He has no idea what it is, but he agrees he is in debt. Jaggers, on behalf of Pip's donor, gives him a present of £500 with the news that he will receive the same amount annually until his benefactor presents himself. When that will be, though, he has no idea.

Pip waits in Wemmick's office for Jaggers who is to dine at Barnard's Inn. He asks Wemmick's advice on helping a friend to get launched in business, but Wemmick is unenthusiastic, saying the official view could not support it, adding, as always, that he should 'invest in portable property'.

They all leave the office together, Pip wishing that Wemmick was dining with him instead of Jaggers.

If you have considered that, up to this point, Pip has been a fairly unpleasant person, you will now see a change. For the first time since he came to London, he is thinking about someone else in a practical way. He wants to help Herbert and this is his first thought when he receives his generous birthday gift.

## CHAPTER 37, *pp. 311–18*

The following Sunday Pip calls on Wemmick to discuss futher the possibility of helping Herbert to get launched in business. He spends a few minutes with Aged Parent while waiting for Wemmick to come in. Miss Skiffins is with him. It is not long before Pip realizes Wemmick's lady-friend is a regular visitor at the Castle.

Walking round with Wemmick later, he outlines all his reasons for helping Herbert and stresses that it has to be done anonymously (p. 314).

Wemmick thinks it a generous gesture and he is sure Mr Skiffins, an accountant, will assist Pip. He thoroughly enjoys the homeliness of Sunday afternoon and evening at Walworth Castle (well described by Dickens) but he tries not to outstay his welcome, and leaves before Miss Skiffins.

A week later there has been some progress, so Pip returns. There are further meetings after that, both at Walworth and in London, until finally negotiations are completed. Herbert comes home to Barnard's Inn in a state of great excitement.

He tells Pip that he has at last found an opening (p. 317). He is to work with Clarriker, a young shipping-broker, and there is a real chance that he will become a partner. Pip is overjoyed to see him so happy and to know he has been able to help.

## CHAPTER 38, *pp. 318–30*

Pip and Estella are often together these days, yet their relationship does not progress, nor does it afford them any happiness either. She uses him, abuses him, reminds him regularly that they have been forced upon each other, and that she has no feelings.

One day this is demonstrated in an unexpected way. They have just arrived at Satis House. Miss Havisham does not like Estella's aloofness, and she accuses her of being exactly what she is – a cold, heartless, arrogant creature: beautiful, but without emotion.

The melodrama is acted out in Pip's presence and Miss Havisham's voice rises and falls hysterically, in contrast to the evenness of Estella's, who defends herself against all the charges with the final words, 'I must be taken as I have been made' (p. 324). Pip slips out into the garden when Miss Havisham collapses on the floor. When he returns, peace has been restored. They play cards until bedtime. During the night, Miss Havisham, obviously distressed, walks about the room groaning.

The Finches reminds Drummle that he has not toasted a lady, in the tradition of the club, so he proposes the health of Estella. Pip and Herbert react suspiciously and Drummle is charged by the President to provide proof that he knows the lady. Later, when he presents a note in Estella's handwriting, Pip is honour-bound to make a public apology. When he complains to Estella about Drummle, she says she has deceived and entrapped all men, except Pip.

Pip has watched these two unnatural characters – Miss Havisham and Estella – act out their strange, embittered drama yet, despite all that he has seen and all that he knows, he does not expect to be a victim. He is hanging on to the threads of unreality, but is well and truly caught in Miss Havisham's web. So, too, is Estella whose exploitation is apparent to all.

## CHAPTER 39, *pp. 330–42*

It is now a year since Pip and Herbert moved from Barnard's Inn to the Temple. Herbert is away on business abroad, and Pip misses his cheerful company. One wild, stormy night he discovers a stranger on the stairs; little does he realize that his world is about to collapse in ruins.

The man enters, extending his hands as though greeting an old friend, and hailing Pip as 'master', thus acknowledging him as a gentleman. Pip instinctively draws back and while he wonders how to get rid of the unwelcome caller, the man says, 'I'm glad you've grow'd up a game one!'

In a flash, the years melt away and Pip recognizes his convict. Caught off guard, Pip allows his hands to be held and kissed in spite of his revulsion. Magwitch clings to him like a father greeting his long-lost son.

'You acted noble, my boy,' said he. 'Noble, Pip! And I have never forgot it!'

Quite harshly Pip tells him they have little in common, but he adopts a gentler tone when he sees tears in the elderly man's eyes. He learns that his visitor has done well for himself, as a sheep-farmer among other things.

Gradually the disgusting truth emerges. After burning the two one-pound notes that Pip has just returned, Magwitch declares himself Pip's benefactor. When the full horror of his words has begun to sink in, Pip is aghast. His great expectations disappear at a stroke, and the idea that he is beholden to such a vile creature is humiliating and odious. He is numbed by shame and shock and would have fainted had not Magwitch caught him in time.

Magwitch tells Pip that his action on the marshes so impressed him that he swore there and then, that, should he ever regain his freedom and have the chance to make money, he would work hard to make Pip a gentleman. His success is a personal triumph, and he delights in his achievement, completely unaware of the effect it is having on the 'gentleman' he has made.

By now Pip is nearly out of his mind, and when Magwitch speaks of the risks he has taken to visit Pip, Pip is obliged to put him up and provide a hiding-place. After Magwitch has retired to Herbert's room for the night, Pip sits down in a daze. His hopes and aspirations as far as Miss Havisham and Estella are concerned are shattered. But the deepest wound, as well as the most grievous hurt, is what he has done to Joe. He has sacrificed him and severed the 'bonds of fellowship' (see Introduction, p. 24) for a convict's whim and his own false expectations.

This is a powerful, brilliant chapter, full of suspense, mystery, revelation and bitter disappointment: we see at once the climax of the Magwitch drama, and the bathos of the Pip saga. Had you any idea it was Magwitch who provided Pip's money the first time you read the novel? From Pip's childhood days all the 'evidence' pointed to Miss Havisham, even though Jaggers tells him in the next chapter (p. 351) that there was 'not a particle of evidence'.

With his life in ruins, Pip begins to understand that fairy god-mothers do not wave magic wands (p. 183), and that people and things are not always what they seem. He rues the day that he parted from Joe.

Since the opening scene, the Magwitch story has featured only in chapters 3 and 5. Pip has been haunted by his memories of the marshes and his convict, and he has been tainted by prison and crime, but there has been nothing to suggest that Magwitch was responsible for Pip's good fortune.

Magwitch oozes vain pleasure in this chapter. He has taken his revenge on society, and is now the proud 'owner' of a gentleman. Although he wants to hit back at the class system that has abused him, he genuinely desires to do something for Pip. Pip is the only person who has ever shown him any kindness. He does not realize, however, that life is not as simple as that; he cannot take over someone else's life in such a possessive way and expect that person to accept it. It is exploitation again.

The Magwitch story gathers momentum from this point, and the reader is in for several more shocks as he lives through more suspense and tension with Pip. Pip's 'bad side of human nature' is apparent here, but we shall change our opinion of him as his narrative proceeds, and be glad of the reasons for doing so.

This chapter is important because it contains the heart of the book's themes. It is what we are that matters, not what we own or our position in society.

Events have exploded Pip's myth. Gentility is an illusion. Wealth does not equal rank. This is the end of the second stage of Pip's expectations.

## CHAPTER 40, *pp. 342–54*

After a restless night, plagued by disturbing thoughts of his broken life, Pip has to make a decision about his 'dreaded visitor'. He could perhaps introduce him as his uncle 'unexpectedly come from the country'. The presence of someone on the stairs (p. 342) adds to his already considerable burden when the watchman tells him someone else was with his 'uncle' the previous night.

The convict looks, if anything, even worse in daylight. His name is Abel Magwitch, but he is known as Provis. He insists that he has paid for his crimes and that Jaggers has been on his side. Pip is appalled by the greedy way he eats, still 'like a hungry old dog' (cf. p. 50).

Magwitch admits his weaknesses for food and his smoke, which seem to have led him into most of his trouble. He is insensitive to the fact that Pip eats nothing and he beams with renewed pride upon the gentleman he has made.

Magwitch has planned that Pip should have everything that money can buy; as he flings his pocket-book down he says he has come home to see Pip spend money 'like a gentleman'. He curses those who have had a hand in his downfall. His wealth, by now, is abhorrent to Pip; he hates all that is happening. He calls a halt to the convict's wild excitement, and asks some basic questions about the old man's immediate plans. Instinctively, Magwitch knows he has offended Pip, and he says he will not be 'low' again. Pip makes light of it, and arranges to house him close by, kit him out with some kind of disguise, and help him escape discovery. Herbert will also have to be told.

Later, Pip visits Jaggers who confirms that Magwitch is his benefactor. Pip tells Jaggers that he is partly to blame for Pip's coming to the wrong conclusion by his implication that his benefactor was Miss Havisham. Of course, the lawyer denies that there was ever any evidence to suggest this.

When the new clothes arrive the following day, Pip concludes that nothing can possibly disguise Provis. He still looks every inch a convict.

Pip is the prisoner now. In addition to all that has happened to him personally, he has more to worry about. He has a vulgar man under his roof, sleeping in his friend's bed, a man whom he knows only as a violent criminal who petrified him for two days during his childhood. He has no idea what terrible crimes the man has committed – he does not even know if he is completely sane – and now he is alone with him and the hideous wretch is claiming that he has made Pip what he is. His habits repulse Pip; everything about him is nauseating.

But the suspense is still kept up: who was lurking on the stairs, and where has he gone? (See p. 438.)

## CHAPTER 41, *pp. 355–60*

Herbert's reactions to the convict are much the same as Pip's. Magwitch, still insensitive to the effect he is having, repeats his proud boast that he has made Pip a gentleman. It is midnight before Pip can get him to his new lodgings. Pip and Herbert are relieved to be alone at last to discuss their fearful problem.

Pip decides he cannot accept any more money, even though he is still heavily in debt. Herbert suggests there might be some kind of work at Clarriker's (after Pip has told him his desperate thought of becoming a soldier); Pip smiles to himself because Herbert has no idea where the money for that original venture came from.

Even more worrying is the criminal nature of Pip's benefactor. Herbert wonders what reaction Pip could expect if he thwarted any of the convict's plans. Pip wonders whether Magwitch might give himself up and then he (Pip) would feel like a murderer.

After breakfast next morning, Magwitch agrees to tell his story, and emphasizes that he has paid the price of his crimes.

This chapter is important because it shows Herbert's staunch support of Pip. Notice the way they link arms, pace the carpet and make decisions. He gives sound advice and promises, come what may, they will 'see it out together, dear boy'.

## CHAPTER 42, *pp. 360–67*

Magwitch tells his sorry tale. His earliest memory is of stealing turnips and being abandoned by his father. Homeless and alone he had had to do the best he could, but his was a story of 'in jail, out of jail'.

About twenty years earlier, Magwitch had been introduced to a so-called gentleman named Compeyson who offered to change his luck by taking him into partnership: a crooked business it was, too. He should have been warned because this rogue had an accomplice, Arthur, and when Magwitch joined Compeyson, Arthur was dying, haunted by the crimes they had committed. He was taken in by Compeyson, just as Arthur had been.

The callous man used Magwitch in his corrupt business, and abandoned him five years later after they had both been arrested.

Magwitch has no reason to know who the 'rich lady' is (p. 362) nor that she has adopted his daughter.

You will notice that he says 'My Missis' (p. 364), and then stops. The truth about Molly is revealed later (pp. 403, 419).

## CHAPTER 43, *pp. 367–72*

Pip thinks ironically about the great gulf between Estella and Magwitch. He fears that Compeyson will have his revenge and rid himself of his enemy by telling the authorities that Magwitch is in London.

Before taking Magwitch abroad to safety, Pip feels he must see Miss Havisham and Estella. He will be away only a night and on his return Herbert and he will discuss the best tactics. On the pretext of visiting Joe, and leaving Magwitch in Herbert's capable hands, Pip sets off early to Satis House.

En route, he meets Bentley Drummle at the Blue Boar. During their forced conversation the old animosity is revived. Drummle makes a point of mentioning 'the lady' several times and frequently boasts that he will be dining with her, before he rides off 'in his blundering, brutal manner'. Pip makes his way to Satis House in melancholy mood.

Pip recoils from Magwitch but wonders how much of this feeling is directly attributable to his feeling for Estella. (Did you spot the irony in view of the fact that Magwitch is Estella's father?) Pip resolves never to tell Magwitch of his love, but later, when he discovers who Estella really is, and when his feelings for Magwitch have changed, he consoles the old man (p. 470). You should note the good description in this chapter and the humour when Pip meets Drummle.

## CHAPTER 44, *pp. 372–9*

As Pip enters the dilapidated room at Satis House, he is aware of an exchange of looks between Estella, who is knitting at Miss Havisham's feet, and the old lady. (The movements of Estella's hands stay in his memory, as you will discover later, p. 403.)

Pip sits among Miss Havisham's ruined belongings inwardly noting that they suit his present mood. He tells her that she has succeeded in making him as unhappy as she could ever have meant him to be, and then tells her all he has learnt recently, adding that the name of his benefactor must remain a secret.

He supposes that when he had been odd-boy at the forge, he had been hired out and paid as part of Miss Havisham's plan of revenge. When he met Mr Jaggers at Satis House and wrongly assumed that Miss Havisham intended to improve his lot, she had encouraged that misunderstanding and he does not think that was at all kind. Miss Havisham explodes with rage and shouts that she can see no reason why she should have been kind. Her sudden outburst causes Estella to look at her in surprise.

Pip accepts that he has been well paid for his visits, and quickly changes the subject to talk about the Hammersmith Pockets. He begs that she change her opinion of both Matthew and Herbert as he believes she has misjudged them. They cannot be compared with the rest of the Pocket family because they at least are genuine. He asks her to consider providing Herbert with some money secretly because Pip, in his present predicament, is unable to continue the anonymous payments that he began two years previously.

He then turns to Estella and confesses that had it not been for 'his long mistake' in believing that Miss Havisham intended them for each other, he would have told her long ago how much he loves her. She tells him yet again that she is incapable of feeling love, but that plans are in hand for her to marry Drummle. Pip implores her to seek out a better partner, and in his bitter distress at losing her, says he could bear it more if she would only find someone worthier. She obviously thinks nothing of Bentley Drummle, and tells Pip that she will not make him happy. Pip cannot bear to think of her as Bentley's wife. Seeing his anguish, she, who knows nothing of feelings, assures

Pip that he will get over it in time; but Pip knows that because Estella is 'part of his existence', he will never forget her.

'All done, all gone!' So desperate is Pip that he cannot face anyone. He decides to walk home (see p. 509 n.), a distance of twenty-six miles, and, when he reaches the outer gate, the night-porter gives him a note from Wemmick. It reads, 'Don't go home.'

Pip is paying a very high price for his arrogance and snobbery, even though we might consider it serves him right when we remember how much he has hurt Joe.

His world is in ruins and now, in his desperation, he suffers the humiliation of tears (p. 377) as he learns of Estella's wedding plans. Is he beginning to understand that she is incapable of warmth and affection? Did you notice after his poetic confession of love (p. 378) how the words affected her? She was amazed at the fluency, the picturesque speech and the agony of his expression. *But she felt nothing.* Miss Havisham has done a perfect job. She has brought the girl up to be hard and she should have been ecstatic to hear Pip's love so eloquently expressed. But she is not gloating. Pip has brought out something from the depth of her being that she had forgotten was there. Her hand is covering her heart reminding her of her broken 'romance', but there is a hint of 'pity and remorse' now.

This chapter is important because now that the deception is over Pip can speak the truth to Estella and Miss Havisham. Later, after that long walk, he is ready to face up to reality.

## CHAPTER 45, *pp. 379–86*

Pip takes a cab to Hummums, a dingy, insect-infested hotel where he can be sure of a bed, but not so sure about the people who have slept in it. He is in no mood for sleep. In his mind's eye he sees Estella – all her looks and tones – and the manner of their parting cuts deep. Running through his restless thoughts during the long night are fears about why he should not go home, and when at last he falls into a fitful sleep, Wemmick's message still haunts him.

Next morning his worst fears about Compeyson are realized. When he calls at Walworth Wemmick tells him his premises have been watched and rumours are circulating that Magwitch has left Australia. Wemmick arranges for Magwitch to be moved to safer lodgings, off the beaten-track, with Herbert's fiancée.

It is unsafe for Pip to visit Magwitch, except before he returns home that day.

Wemmick's legal training makes caution his second nature so, although they are at Walworth in their 'private and personal capacities' he names no names. Instead, he refers to (p. 384) 'Tom, Jack or Richard' when he means Magwitch. You should be able to find another name for Magwitch, and other expressions for Newgate and Australia, on p. 382.

## CHAPTER 46, *pp. 387–94*

Pip makes his way to Mill Pond Bank where he finds Magwitch in comfortable rooms at the top of the house. He tells him that in the interests of his safety Wemmick has suggested they go abroad. To avoid suspicion, Herbert thinks it a good idea if he and Pip row Magwitch down the river at the appropriate time; in the meantime, Pip can take up rowing so that it will seem normal for him to be engaged in it. Both Pip and Magwitch approve of the plan, and it is arranged that as Pip rows past Mill Pond Bank, Magwitch will pull down his blind as a sign he has seen him and everything is all right. Herbert will make the direct contact because it is normal for him to visit Clara. Magwitch is now known as Mr Campbell, and Herbert tells Mrs Whimple that the lodger has been entrusted to him and must be well cared for.

On Pip's way home, thoughts of Clara lead to thoughts of Estella and he becomes sad. He organizes his boat and is soon practising regularly, sometimes with Herbert, sometimes alone. Before long his presence on the river is taken for granted, and no one makes any comment.

The signals are positive and all is well, but Pip has misgivings. He feels he is always being watched and he fears for Magwitch's safety.

## CHAPTER 47, *pp. 394–400*

It is a miserable time for Pip. There has been no news from Wemmick for weeks, he is short of money, upset about Estella's marriage (he even refuses to accept it as fact) but, above all, he lives in fear and dread of Magwitch's discovery. All he can do is row and wait, and he grows more and more depressed.

He decides to cheer himself up one evening by going to the theatre. Wopsle is acting in a patriotic naval comedy followed by a comic pantomime. During the show, Mr Wopsle stares at Pip and waits for him at the door afterwards. Pip greets him politely and is surprised when Wopsle asks who is with him. Ever mindful of traps Pip says nothing, but his fear returns and he glances suspiciously about while Wopsle goes on talking. He recalls the Christmas Day when they joined in the chase of the convicts on the marshes, and Wopsle tells Pip that he has just seen the one with the disfigured face, sitting behind him in the theatre. Pip keeps his head and gives nothing away to Wopsle, though his racing heart and sudden pallor reveal his alarm at the news.

The suspense is building up now. Compeyson is obviously following Pip so that he can find Magwitch. Pip will take extra precautions.

## CHAPTER 48, *pp. 400–407*

A week later Jaggers invites Pip to dine with him. Wemmick is there, too, but on his official behaviour which keeps Pip at a distance. During the meal, Pip confirms he will visit Miss Havisham the next day. She has asked to see him on 'a little matter of business' and has sent a note via Jaggers. When the lawyer starts to talk about Estella's marriage, and 'putting a case' about its outcome, Pip is far from happy.

Molly, the housekeeper, is nervous when Jaggers speaks to her. Pip stares at her fingers and a strange feeling comes over him such as he has had on previous occasions (pp. 235, 289, 403). Memories of Estella's eyes, fingers and hair fill his mind and he suddenly knows that this woman with similar eyes, fingers and hair is Estella's mother.

Wemmick and Pip leave together, and as soon as they are out of earshot, Wemmick becomes friendly and relaxed. He speaks highly of Jaggers, as usual, but explains that he cannot relax in his company; Pip agrees. Pip is curious to know more about the housekeeper, and Wemmick says he will tell what he knows 'in our private and personal capacities, of course'. He tells the story summarized in our Synopsis (but Wemmick does not know that 'the tramping man' is Magwitch) and gives details about how Jaggers tied everyone up in knots during the case, and proved that Molly was too weak to have strangled anyone. It was all too much for the judge and jury, so Molly was acquitted.

'All done, all gone! So much was done and gone . . .' (p. 378) says Pip. And for what? He has sacrificed Joe, Biddy, home, and his self-respect. The irony of it all! The young 'lady' is not what she seems and her background is more 'coarse and common' than Pip's. So much for wealth, material possessions and education. Gentility is none of these things.

## CHAPTER 49, *pp. 407–15*

When Pip visits Satis House, he is astounded by the change in Miss Havisham. After a life numbed by isolation and self-inflicted misery, feeling seems to be returning. She gives Pip a note for Jaggers authorizing the anonymous payment of £900 into Herbert's business, and offers Pip money, too; but he is past accepting any.

She wants forgiveness and to make amends for the lives she has ruined. Pip loses no time in forgiving her in spite of all that he has suffered on account of her bitterness. It is too late to regret the past and he encourages Miss Havisham to save Estella from further distress.

All the time Miss Havisham is hysterical, crying over and over and over again 'What have I done!'. Before he leaves, Pip finds out the circumstances of Estella's arrival at Satis House. They part and Pip takes a last nostalgic look around; in the brewery he experiences the same premonition that he remembers from his childhood (pp. 94, 413). Running back to Miss Havisham, he finds her ablaze. He struggles to smother the flames and sits with her until early next morning. A surgeon dresses her wounds and arranges for her bed to be made up on the great table (see p. 116). Pip kisses her and takes his leave just as she is muttering the third of her oft-repeated three sentences, '. . . I forgive her'.

Miss Havisham's story is nearly over. Did she attempt suicide?

# CHAPTER 50, *pp. 416–19*

Pip's hands and left arm are heavily bandaged and this puts paid to his rowing practice for a while. The burns are extremely painful, but, even worse, he is haunted by visions of the flames and Miss Havisham. While he changes the dressings, Herbert talks about Magwitch.

He adds to the story that Wemmick has told Pip about Molly (p. 405), picking up Magwitch's own story where he broke off (p. 364) about his Missis. When he has finished, Pip tells Herbert that Magwitch is Estella's father.

Herbert's genuine friendship shines through this episode. While he is telling the story, he is busily dressing the wounds and doing his best not to hurt Pip. We can anticipate Pip's illness by Herbert's concern about his irregular breathing. Another thing to anticipate is Herbert's marriage which cannot be too far off.

Herbert has also heard from Magwitch that Compeyson knew all about the trial and forced him to work hard, and cheated him out of his just dues.

Think what Pip has surrendered in his quest to raise his status high enough to impress Estella, whose mother was a prostitute and father a vagrant.

## CHAPTER 51, *pp. 420–27*

Pip visits Little Britain, mainly to have facts about Molly and Magwitch confirmed. He is glad to find Wemmick and Jaggers in the same office, because Wemmick can hear his account first hand and thus know that Pip has not betrayed his earlier confidence (see p. 405).

Jaggers, in his usual disinterested way, listens without comment, but Pip is sharp enough to note that he obviously does not know that Magwitch is Estella's father. When Pip has told all he knows, Jaggers tries to resume his work with Wemmick, but Pip demands some consideration after all he has suffered as the result of his 'false hopes'. Jaggers remains unmoved, so Pip appeals to Wemmick, as a man of feeling, to speak to Jaggers on his behalf. Jaggers is staggered to hear that Wemmick has 'pleasant and playful ways' (p. 424) and Wemmick is embarrassed that his Walworth secrets are revealed.

Jaggers puts 'the case' as is his custom when he is stating facts. Pip learns that Molly had had to tell her lawyer about the child and he – knowing what hopeless lives children of his clients led – had bargained for the child's adoption. Jaggers hints that no possible good could come from disclosing these facts to any of those involved.

This is a key chapter for Jaggers and shows how he links all three stories. Pip has now solved all the mysteries, but the story is far from over.

## CHAPTER 52, *pp. 427–32*

Pip completes the business with Clarriker and feels deeply satisfied.

At last he hears from Wemmick that the Magwitch escape bid can begin in forty-eight hours (note Wemmick's caution again). As Pip is still handicapped, Herbert suggests Startop should row. They draw up detailed plans, make careful arrangements and take the necessary precautions.

A mysterious note arrives summoning Pip to the marshes and, thinking it might help Magwitch's escape, he decides to go. He is not recognized at the inferior inn where he first stays, and the landlord tells him the story of the ungrateful young man who rose in the world, but who has since ignored his 'earliest benefactor and the founder of his fortunes', namely Pumblechook! Pip's thoughts turn nostalgically to Joe, 'long-suffering and loving Joe', and he is unable to finish his supper.

One of the saving graces in Pip's life now is that he has helped his good friend, Herbert. He keeps it a secret, and listens as Herbert tells him all about his plans for the firm's expansion – and his wedding.

Pip's concern for Miss Havisham makes him find time to inquire after her while his meal is being prepared at the inn (p. 431) and he is filled with remorse again remembering Joe's goodness.

Pip's other saving grace is his anxiety for Magwitch. Ever at the back of his mind is the plan for his benefactor's safety and now that he has stopped being self-centred, a true gentleman is emerging. A gentleman cares about the feelings and well-being of others, and is motivated by the ideas and values of chivalry.

## CHAPTER 53, *pp. 432–44*

Orlick has been following Pip's movements for some time and knows about his 'Uncle Provis' and the plot to get him out of the country. Enjoying his revenge, Orlick mentions 'new companions and new masters' (p. 438) and spits out details of Compeyson's evil intentions to prevent Magwitch's escape and send him to the gallows.

Pip has been securely tied to a ladder. Orlick gloats over his prisoner and picks up the gun which Pip recognizes (p. 255). Jealously, he reveals the grudges he has harboured against Pip (pp. 435–6) and also describes what he did to Pip's sister (p. 437) and how it was he lurking on the stairs (p. 438).

Suddenly, in a drunken frenzy, he picks up a stone hammer. Simultaneously Pip shouts and kicks with all his strength; that is the last he knows, and the last he expects to know. He is saved by a highly dramatic intervention.

Herbert has found Orlick's letter at home and guided by Trabb's boy has tracked Pip down. He manages to save him. Back in London, Pip spends Tuesday in bed trying to get himself well enough for Wednesday's great task. He is almost out of his mind with worry lest his ill-health upset the arrangements – or Compeyson denounce Magwitch. Eventually he sleeps and by next morning is well enough to face the day.

The author's sense of the over-dramatic is exciting in this chapter. He begins by setting the scene, and his choice of words makes us anticipate some of the tension that follows. 'It was a *dark night*'; 'there was a *melancholy wind* and the marshes were *very dismal*'; '. . . they [the marshes] were so oppressive that I hesitated, half inclined to go back'. And the ominous words, '. . . having come there *against my inclination*, I went on *against it*'. (The italics are mine.)

If we were televizing the scene, the camera would focus on the isolated limekiln, and the flickering light in the deserted old sluice-house. It would pick out images that show the desolation, the dilapidation and the darkness and it would film the vapour from the kiln creeping 'in a ghostly way' towards Pip. Perhaps we should catch a distorted glimpse of the evil Orlick waiting in the shadows to pounce. The stage is set for the melodrama to begin.

Here is another character getting his revenge. Orlick has been jealous of Pip for years. Now he is going to make him suffer in a macabre way. The ingredients of horror are well mixed, and as he threatens to murder Pip, and dispose of his body without trace, he all but burns him with the candle.

Pip's thoughts in this chapter are worth careful study.

## CHAPTER 54, *pp. 444–57*

The plan of escape is for Pip's friends to row with the tide for six hours, against it until nightfall, put up for the night and board a steamer on Thursday. Pip is relieved to be on the way and 'the movement of the river', 'the moving river' and 'the road that ran with them' are symbolic of his optimism on that eventful day.

Magwitch is waiting at the appointed place, and he greets Pip gratefully as they take him on board. All goes well until they find an inferior inn for the night. Pip's worst fears are realized then, when he hears that the river-police are about (pp. 451–2). Pip and company hold an emergency meeting, and decide to lie low next day until the last minute. All their plans are to no avail.

At half-past one the steamer is in view, but at the same moment the river-police appear from nowhere and are soon alongside shouting orders for the arrest of Magwitch. Pandemonium follows. Magwitch is arrested as the two boats spin round together. As he leans across to identify the cloaked Compeyson, both convicts go overboard.

Later, the badly-injured Magwitch is rescued and manacled; there is no sign of Compeyson. Back at the inn where they had spent the previous night, Magwitch tells Pip how he had struggled with his enemy under water, escaped and swum away, but had injured his head under the steamer's keel and his chest 'against the side of the galley'.

The police confiscate Magwitch's belongings which include the pocket-book, and Pip is permitted to accompany him to London. They are returning to the grim, hard world where even seriously wounded, reformed convicts cannot expect any compassion, and Pip knows he can never desert Magwitch. Magwitch had come back for Pip's sake and the least he can do is to promise affection and loyalty to this 'hunted, wounded, shackled creature'. They hold hands in the boat and Pip hears the emotional click in the old man's throat.

The description of the trip down the river is nothing less than a masterpiece. The inward eye focuses on one vivid image after another, and the inward ear listens to the sounds of the restless movement of the river.

How do you feel about Magwitch? Does he deserve all this suffering? At least Pip is behaving as a true friend and the old man has the consolation that someone cares about him at last. Pip says (p. 456) his 'repugnance to him had all melted away'. We can say the same thing about our feelings towards Pip.

All his falseness has disappeared. He tells Magwitch, 'I will be as true to you, as you have been to me!' – and he means it.

## CHAPTER 55, *pp. 458–65*

Jaggers says Magwitch's case is hopeless, and Pip insists that his benefactor should be told about his legacy being forfeited to the Crown. He does not want Magwitch to be disillusioned.

Before he leaves for Cairo, Herbert extends an open invitation to Pip to join him as a clerk in the office and to share his home when he marries Clara. Pip is moved, but asks for time to consider.

Wemmick calls to explain that he had tried to give Pip good advice but Compeyson had been too clever for them. He regrets the loss of the 'portable property' more that the fate of the owner because there is no hope for Magwitch, but there could have been hope for riches. He invites Pip 'to take a walk' the following Monday and, although Pip does not feel up to it, he agrees, considering all that Wemmick has done for him. He has a pleasant surprise on the day when he realizes he is to be best man at Wemmick's wedding.

What do you think the 'vague something' is in Pip's thoughts (p. 460)? (Answer on p. 481.) This wedding is a humorous interlude in the midst of the gloom and pathos.

## CHAPTER 56, *pp. 465–70*

On account of his reputation as a hardened criminal, Magwitch should have been clapped in irons, but because he is so ill he is imprisoned in the infirmary. At the Sessions, he and thirty-one other convicts are sentenced to death and Pip holds his hand while judgement is pronounced. Magwitch replies, 'My Lord, I have received my sentence of Death from the Almighty, but I bow to yours.'

All Pip can do now is to appeal against the judgement, and he writes several letters to notable people. Magwitch's health deteriorates rapidly, but one day he makes a final effort to rally and thanks Pip for sticking by him. He is close to death, and it is then that Pip consoles him by telling of his own love for the child that Magwitch had 'loved and lost' (p. 470). The old man presses and kisses Pip's hand just before he dies peacefully – his thirst for someone to relate to quenched.

## CHAPTER 57, *pp. 470–82*

The debt collectors arrive to arrest Pip who is now without prospects, his great expectations having been destroyed, but he is too ill (after the events of the past two months) to be moved. His fever lasts several weeks and when the crisis is over he finds at his bedside dear, loyal Joe. Biddy has sent him.

Joe tells Pip that Miss Havisham has died and left her estate to Estella with the exception of 'a cool £4,000' which she has left to Matthew Pocket – at Pip's request – and small amounts to the other Pockets. Orlick is in jail after assaulting Pumblechook and robbing him.

Joe nurses Pip back to health and treats him with all the care and love that he had known in his childhood. As he recovers, Joe's embarrassed formality returns and Pip wonders how to recapture the old Joe. He decides that the day after next (Monday) he will tell Joe everything, and his future plans. They can then pick up their old relationship. They spend a quiet Sunday together, but by Monday Joe has gone, leaving a note and a receipt for Pip's debt. Pip loses his chance to tell Joe of his plans to marry Biddy.

Joe's love shows, in spite of all he has suffered from Pip, that he bears him no grudge. He remembers nothing but his love for Pip. Pip recognizes in Joe 'a gentle Christian man' (p. 472) and understands the futility of his artificial idea of a gentleman.

This chapter is important because it demonstrates the sincerity of a genuine relationship. Joe, whose marriage is imminent by the time Pip recovers, has dropped everything to nurse him back to health. Pip is bitterly ashamed of the way he has hurt Joe: 'O Joe, you break my heart!' (p. 472).

## CHAPTER 58, *pp. 482–9*

Pip travels home to thank Joe and to seek Biddy's hand. He has a cool reception at the Blue Boar now that he is poor again. After returning from Satis House, which he discovers is up for sale, he finds Pumblechook waiting for him in the coffee-room. He is as obnoxious as ever and gives Pip a message for Joe which makes little sense to Pip, but which inflates Pumblechook's ego.

Approaching his old home, Pip feels glad anticipation, but he wonders why the school is closed and the forge silent. There is another shock in store. The house is alive and cheerful with flowers and Joe and Biddy – dressed in their best – greet him with open arms. It is their wedding day and Pip's first feeling is of tremendous relief that he did not tell Joe of his plans. He is delighted for both of them, thanks them for everything, and asks to be forgiven for all the hurt he has caused them both. After a happy meal together, Pip leaves them to themselves and returns to London.

Later, he works happily in Herbert's office and lives with Herbert and Clara (who were married four months after his arrival in Cairo) and eventually becomes a partner in the firm. Clarriker at last tells Herbert the secret that Pip has kept all these years: that Pip had been responsible for arranging Herbert's partnership, and had even enlisted Miss Havisham's help when his financial expectations collapsed.

This chapter is important because at last Pip confesses the difference between true and false values. He honours Joe and Biddy because they are 'both so good and true'.

## CHAPTER 59, *pp. 489–93*

Eleven years later, Pip returns to the forge. Joe and Biddy have two children, one of whom is named Pip 'for your sake, dear old chap', says Joe. Biddy tells him he should marry, but Pip says he will remain a bachelor – he thinks, too, that his dream about Estella has gone. He has heard that Bentley Drummle died in an accident, but not before he had treated his wife abominably; Pip wonders whether she has remarried.

For old times' sake, he visits the site of Satis House where he has an unexpected, but promising, reunion with Estella; she has changed considerably and is glad to see him. They pledge friendship to each other, and Pip takes her hand.

Now they accept each other unconditionally, there is some hope for their relationship. Did you notice how Pip remembers Magwitch when he takes his daughter's 'once insensible hand'?

Originally, Dickens ended his novel on p. 490 (see Appendix A, pp. 494–6) but ever since he changed it and added chapter 59, there has been an argument about which is the better conclusion and why. You will have to make up your own mind. We can agree though, that Pip has grown wiser through suffering and caring, and that he is finally 'a gentleman at heart' (p. 204). There is no higher tribute.

# Characters

## PIP

'Conscience is a dreadful thing when it accuses man or boy . . .' (p. 44) reflects the adult Pip, but conscience has been his blessing in disguise.

We have felt kindly towards Pip as a small lad and many times we have smiled at his guilty conscience. You cannot have forgotten, for example, 'the black ox with a white cravat on' that reminds him of the clergyman, and prompts the involuntary, tearful explanation from Pip, clutching his swag, 'I couldn't help it, sir! It wasn't for myself I took it!' (p. 48). A youngster does not change fundamentally, whatever stages he goes through in life. Pip will go seriously astray as he grows up, but the power of his conscience will finally return him to his boyhood honesty and goodness.

Pip's happy relationship with Joe is the one bright feature of his otherwise dark childhood. 'Home had never been a very pleasant place to me, because of my sister's temper. But, Joe had sanctified it . . .' (p. 134). It is not hard to understand the terrors that life holds for this imaginative, sensitive child. Nor is it surprising that he is tempted by the chance of a different life.

Miss Havisham seems to provide that chance on the first day Pip visits Satis House. Once aware that he is 'coarse and common' life can never be the same again. Pip cannot accept himself as he is (p. 94, last six lines) and by the end of the day he is frustrated and ashamed of Joe and of home, too (p. 101).

Pip's notion of a gentleman, like all men's Utopias, is as insubstantial as his own shadow, but he chases it all the same. He thinks that being a gentleman means having money, fine clothes, servants – material things. He does not realize it also means having a true heart and real feelings for all other people. Suddenly Jaggers – a link with Satis House – is there telling him about his great expectations and it is all happening to him. He thinks his fairy-tale is coming true, but, like all fairy-tales, it does not come true.

Things and people are not always what they seem. Neither are places: London is disappointing. 'There at the very core of London, in the heart of its business and animation, stemming the giant currents of life that flow ceaselessly on from different quarters and meet beneath its walls: stands Newgate.' Dickens transfers his own first impressions to Pip when he first views Newgate (p. 189). The prison is symbolic and the 'taint of prison and crime' is to be an immutable part of his life because he has come to London thanks to a convict's money and has given his heart to the same convict's daughter. Magwitch's name shows us his nature; Miss Havisham waves her stick like a wand. The magic each creates is an illusion, and London is the place of lies where their magic sends Pip.

Corruption is all around him, beginning in Jaggers's office where Pip receives his allowance and instructions. It pursues him on his way to meet Estella (pp. 248, 280). Seeing the chained convicts reminds him of Magwitch and takes the edge off his excitement about Estella, filling his mind instead with misgivings (p. 252). His visit to Newgate stirs up similar feelings. The illusions of London are always close to crime.

Try as he may, Pip cannot shake himself free. Vague worries lurk at the back of his mind when he sees Molly (pp. 235, 403); fears and uncertainties possess him in Estella's company (pp. 259, 284, 289). Happiness always eludes him and his conscience often reminds him of Joe (e.g. pp. 258, 265, 291, 341). The 'fairy tale' life of the false gentleman is full of pain rather than the pleasure he dreams of.

It takes Pip only one day to remove himself in distance and class from 'the poor old kitchen' of his former life (p. 208).

Before we judge Pip too harshly, we must remember that his background hardly prepares him for affluence, and its power goes straight to his head. Idle living, extravagant spending, and dreams of Estella fill his days uselessly until his arrogance, conceit and shallowness make him unbearable.

Biddy's letter is an intrusion and Joe's proposed visit an embarrassment. He has gone a long way downhill since he told Joe he would never forget him (p. 174), but his conscience will not let him get away with it.

Nor will his conscience let him enjoy his fairy-tale life with its sham values, but our gentleman of fortune conjures up excuses to cheat himself whenever he can. 'All other swindlers upon earth are nothing to the self-swindlers' (p. 247), but conscience never disappears completely, and Pip has regrets and nostalgic thoughts about Joe, the forge and Biddy, and knows he would have been a better person without Miss Havisham's influence (p. 291).

One unselfish act redeems him during the worst phase of his life, and that is his anonymous generosity to his good friend, Herbert; this includes going cap in hand to Miss Havisham when his own source of income has dried up (pp. 309, 313–14, 317, 375).

Dreams and pretence cannot last for ever, so when the personification of 'the taint of prison and crime' turns up, Pip is faced with the 'sober reality' of Magwitch. In the final section of the book, Pip moves off the centre of his stage and into the wings. Thus his moral recovery begins.

It is in the sluice-house that we can see the real Pip who has shed the impostor's garment. Other people are more important by then. Pip's generous nature has already forgiven Miss Havisham, in spite of his ruined chances and expectations (p. 410). He cares personally for Magwitch who has risked and done so much for him; if he dies, Herbert will doubt his integrity and believe he abandoned Magwitch. Above all, Biddy and Joe, those two saintly people, would never know how sorry he was, or how true he had meant to be (p. 436). At death's door his greatest fear is being misremembered, but he need have no fears.

Pip survives the threat to his life. Magwitch becomes the first duty of his life (p. 465) and Pip's latent humanity reappears, reminding him that Magwitch is a far better man than Pip has ever been to Joe (p. 457). 'Please God, I will be as true to you, as you have been to me!' he says with all the devotion of a loving son to his father, and he keeps his word.

The imposter who once uttered the hollow words (p. 304) to Joe 'I shall be down soon, and often', has gone for good. Next time they meet, Joe is nursing Pip back to health as though nothing has happened or changed, and Pip – penitent and stripped of all falseness – whispers 'O God bless this gentle Christian man' (p. 472), thus taking to his heart all that Joe stands for, and acknowledging all that he had taught Pip in the warmth and security of the forge kitchen.

When he meets Estella again eleven years later, there is real hope of a lasting relationship. Pip's infatuation has given way to mature, true feeling and he is ready to care for her for her own sake, and also for Magwitch's.

## ABEL MAGWITCH also known as
## PROVIS (p. 345) and MR CAMPBELL (p. 392)

Our first encounter with Magwitch hardly suggests that we shall later feel compassion for such a grotesque creature. His all-powerful, petrifying presence dwarfs everything else, leaving the unsightly image of his tattered figure to haunt the reader and narrator alike. What is he up to, we want to know. Where has he come from and who is he? We are secretly glad that he is recaptured before he can harm Pip. Had we known more about him we should have had kinder thoughts, but Dickens intends us to feel abhorrence.

Magwitch is but a blot on the pages of history, a social outcast about whom nobody cares. The things we take for granted such as shelter, food, clothing and being wanted were not part of his childhood, so he grew up in the tradition of the criminal class 'tramping, begging, thieving, working sometimes' (p. 361), with the inevitable consequence of being in and out of jail repeatedly.

The abject isolation, dirt and despair of such a life is hard to imagine, and we should not blame Magwitch for finding what comfort he can. If he jumped 'over the broomstick' (p. 405) to enjoy a false marriage with Molly, good luck to him. How can a man know what standards to live by when he has been hounded by society for the best part of his life?

When we look into his story and remember the loss of the child he loved (p. 406), the vile Compeyson at work (pp. 67–8, 364f, 419, 461) and the prejudiced judge (p. 365), we can sympathize with his loathing of the hierarchy that well-nigh suffocated his spirit, and understand his vow to revenge himself on Compeyson.

It makes sense, too, of his great expectation to make his own gentleman. Does he feel sorry for the small boy who risks so much to feed him? Probably. But it is more than that. Pip brings 'into his mind, the little girl so tragically lost . . .' (p. 419), because she would have been about the same age. He understands the sign Pip makes – the unspoken word that passes between them after his recapture (p. 69) – and at that moment he finds a reason for living. This explains the convict's unexpected confession to the theft at the forge. He has a purpose in life now, and a secret ambition.

Every moment in Australia is devoted to this obsessive desire. In his mind's eye he lives and relives the moment when he will greet his 'gentleman' – the happy embrace, grasping of hands, smiles and celebrations. One wickedly wild night some sixteen years later he is able to say, 'You acted noble, my boy, . . . and I have never forgot it!' (p. 334).

Is it really gratitude for all that Pip has done? Superficially it is, but there is a deeper reason, too. Do you remember the fuss on the coach when a gentleman objected to travelling with two convicts (p. 249) because they were the lowest of the low? Now supposing a convict could make a blacksmith's boy a gentleman – what revenge!

How could anyone so poor, so illiterate, so much a criminal make a fortune? He comes back into Pip's life still every inch a convict, this rough, weather-beaten, muscular man with the furrowed, bald head. His long iron-grey side hair and large veinous hands suggest a man of about sixty. His voice is coarse and the emotional click still sounds in his throat. Apart from Pip's fortune, his pathetic bits and pieces of worldly goods amount to a black pipe (which he fills with labourer's tobacco) a black Testament, his dog-eared playing cards, and a loathsome jack-knife which he sticks into his food, the table and probably anyone who threatens him (p. 354).

Pip hates what he sees and the reader is not sure about him at first either. What about Magwitch? His elation is absolute. He has done what he intended to do. That Pip should feel disgust is the farthest thought from his mind.

Is not Dickens saying that love and kindness will work miracles? Both Magwitch and Pip become better people for knowing and loving each other. Facing 'sober reality' brings out the best in both of them, but they know there cannot be a happy ending. Dickens has made his point, so the evil underworld, in the shape of Compeyson, can have the last word, but Compeyson will 'tumble on the tides' (p. 458) for his trouble.

As Magwitch reveals more about himself, we see he is not the terrifying convict that we thought, but a poor, hounded creature, starved of affection who has been denied basic human rights. As he stands before the judge the prisoner knows he is near to death and his final words to the court (p. 467) are said with moving dignity and pathos.

Not long after that, at peace with the world and happy in the knowledge that his daughter is alive and Pip loves her, he presses Pip's hand for the last time. He dies enjoying a sense of belonging at last to someone who cares. All he ever wanted in the first place was someone to care about him.

Magwitch, as his name suggests, has been a creator of illusion, and, as such, has made an important contribution to the theme that people and things are not always what they seem.

## JOE GARGERY

Joe represents constant values in a fickle society. Black is black and white is white and the only time he allows himself a touch of grey is to cheer up Mrs Joe after she has been on an alarming 'Rampage' over Pip's indentures (pp. 126, 131). Otherwise there is no deviation; 'lies is lies' (p. 100). 'Live well and die happy' is his advice to Pip, and his own great expectation. That he should marry the excellent Biddy is an unexpected reward.

Joe takes his wife's blows (e.g. p. 43) philosophically and with quiet dignity, remembering how his mother had suffered at the hands of his cruel father. This is not weakness but inner strength (p. 40). He could put her in her place (remember Orlick?, p. 142) but he chooses not to, and is rewarded when she recognizes his true worth just before she dies (p. 302).

He sees the world through blue eyes that often track Mrs Joe, trying to understand her Rampages and violence. His smooth face is usually calm, his manner long-suffering. When he is thinking or worried about something, he rubs his 'flaxen curls and whisker' (p. 42) or smokes his pipe (pp. 138, 172). He is a man of habit, happiest in his working-clothes and the familiar surroundings of the Three Jolly Bargemen or his own fireside (pp. 54, 127, 246, 301).

How must he have felt when he suffered that dreadful breakfast with the heartless Pip (p. 241 f)? A casual observer might think him an idiot, but his inner strength is at work again. He blames himself for any fault and puts it down to unfamiliar surroundings and un-comfortable clothes, but the truth is that Pip is no gentleman. Had he been so, Joe would have been more relaxed, and there would have been no need for 'Sir' or apologies. Poor Joe! We can be sure of his inner sorrow even though he 'never complained of anything . . . but ever did his duty in his way of life, with a strong hand, a quiet tongue, and a gentle heart' (p. 303).

The reader should not judge him a fool on account of his unique language. He communicates common sense and has no trouble in making himself understood. It is interesting that he will not speak directly to Miss Havisham who is too unnatural for his way of life (p. 128 f).

In spite of his simplicity, Joe is a force to be reckoned with, and when Jaggers tries to bully him about compensation for Pip, Joe is angry, '. . . if you think as Money can make compensation to me for the loss of the little child – what come to the forge – and ever the best of friends! –' (p. 168). Joe is the only person who stands up to Jaggers *and* makes him retreat! Such folk as he radiate a goodness that money can never contaminate. Joe is ready, too, when the time comes, to clear Pip's debt (p. 481), and there must be more than a touch of self-sacrifice in that gesture.

Pip has so much to thank Joe for (not that he expects thanks): friendship above all else; and the remembrance that Joe has sanctified his home (p. 134) and given him warmth and security in the forge kitchen with his 'Ever the best of friends' (pp. 78, 168, 481), 'what larks' (pp. 240, 472) and 'Pip, old chap' (pp. 43, 472). As a fellow-sufferer, Joe devises ways of taking the lad's mind off the hostility around him. Among other things in their sympathetic relationship, he compares his slice of bread with Pip's (p. 42), mouths words behind Mrs Joe's back (p. 45), shares secrets (p. 53), shows his kindness symbolically in helpings of gravy (p. 57), and does his best to keep Pip 'and Tickler in sunders' (p. 478). Joe invited 'the poor little child' to live at the forge (p. 78) and he became Pip's anchor while he rode out the rough storm of his childhood.

Joe sets the pattern for work and teaches Pip the value of honest toil and faithfulness. His wisdom could have saved the boy much unhappiness, had he taken note. For instance, Joe does not want Pip to return to Satis House (as he has been paid off) in case Miss Havisham thinks he 'expect[s] something of her' (p. 138), but Pip persuades Joe to let him go. Later, Joe sees dangers in Pip's great expectations, so he does not enthuse too much over the news. In fact, the atmosphere at home is quite dismal and Joe, with a hand on each knee, stares into the fire. He will miss Pip, and he fears the boy will be caught up in an artificial life. That is why he tells Biddy 'Pip's a gentleman of fortun' . . .'

Life's disappointments and sorrows do not change Joe. He smokes more (p. 172) when he is about to lose Pip and he cannot finish his familiar sentence at Mrs Joe's funeral '. . . she were a fine figure of a —' (p. 299), but he does not let grief change him as does Miss Havisham. He carries on with his work, and bides his time.

Joe is a great man, strong, simple and pure. How moving it is to see him nursing Pip back to health and picking up the old threads without a word of recrimination (p. 472f).

It seems right that Joe should marry Biddy. They both have the same true standards and will give each other deserved happiness.

## MISS HAVISHAM

If anyone thinks that money brings happiness, look at Miss Havisham and be warned. Cynics will say such a character cannot possibly exist, but most of Dickens's characters are based on real people, and Miss Havisham is no exception (see p. 501).

If Miss Havisham had not been so obstinate at the time, she could have avoided becoming Compeyson's victim. Matthew Pocket could see that he was no gentleman and warned her against 'placing herself too unreservedly in his power' (p. 205), but he saw how difficult it is to get through to someone who is passionately in love.

She is certainly a strange character who provides much of the intrigue in the plot. We want to know what makes a woman so unnatural, so uncanny, so unforgettable. There have been jilted lovers before, but they have lived to fight another day. We can find two clues to her downfall on p. 203 when Herbert begins his story. 'Miss Havisham . . . was a spoilt child. Her mother died when she was a baby, and her father denied her nothing.' She was spoilt and motherless; two handicaps but not enough on their own. Inexperience played a large part, too. This rich heiress had a sheltered upbringing, she was naïve, and used to having everything she wanted from her father. Herbert tells us she had had no romantic relationships before she met Compeyson, so we can imagine how blissfully happy she was, unaware that people and things are not always what they seem.

She was utterly infatuated and had eyes, ears and heart only for her beloved until the letter came. Nothing had been done to prepare her for life's shocks. Not even her money could soften the blow that unbalanced Miss Havisham.

It is at Satis House that we first meet her, one of the strangest of all literary characters, cut off from natural influences and surrounded by the disintegrating relics of the wedding-that-never-was. She sits in the midst of this disintegration, as she has sat for twenty years, 'the strangest lady' still dressed in her faded bridal gown and withered like the flowers pinned to her faded, limp veil. White hair frames her demented face, and her sunken, wild eyes and wrinkled skin remind us that it is a long time since she dressed for her wedding. Soured and sullen, sometimes raving and crazed, she sits in her candlelit prison determined to have her revenge. She is so unnatural that Pip compares her to a skeleton or a waxwork. Her only hope is the pretty little girl she has adopted to 'rear and love'. It becomes her great expectation to steal Estella's heart away and put ice in its place to 'wreak revenge on all the male sex' (pp. 200, 321); for what man will be able to resist such a beauty?

Having brought Estella up to break men's hearts, Miss Havisham works her evil influence on Pip, who is easily caught in her trap. He is captured for about ten years until he has suffered enough to say, 'I am as unhappy as you can ever have meant me to be' (p. 373). Here is a confidence trick worse than Compeyson's. She lures Pip to Satis House, introduces him to her broken heart, plays on his emotions, gives him false expectations, and leads him to believe that even though all men are Estella's victims he will be an exception. Not only does she wreck Pip's young life, but she also exploits Estella and wrecks hers.

Miss Havisham gloats over every conquest Estella makes and loves her greedily and possessively. She wallows in her faultless performance until she is injured by her own scheme. Estella loves no one, not even Miss Havisham. Her heart is stone-cold (p. 322).

Pip uncorks Miss Havisham's bottled-up subconscious. Notice her 'ghastly look' (pp. 377–8) when his heart breaks over Estella. That is just what she wants but his flood of emotion, instead of making her ecstatic in victory, touches something deep within her, producing a shock great enough to bring her back to reality. This time her heart really does break (p. 410).

Even in remorse she is true to her spoilt nature and melodramatically shrieks, drops on her knees, wrings her hands, crushes her hair, and over and over again asks the same question, 'What have I done?' (see ch. 49). She knows what she has done. She has ruined too many lives and there is no escape.

Unless . . . does she try to commit suicide while the balance of her mind is disturbed? She is cleverly named by Dickens. Her life has been a pathetic sham.

## JAGGERS

Everyone is in awe of Jaggers. He makes criminals cringe and free men feel guilty (p. 311) – except Joe, who has clear ideas about right and wrong (p. 168). Money does not rule Joe, but it is Jaggers's life-blood.

For Jaggers time is money and not to be wasted (p. 188). You have to be quick and know your own mind in his company or 'Suddenly – click – you're caught!' (p. 221). He does what he is paid to do, no more, no less. There is no room for sentiment in Jaggers's affairs. He attends to the letter of the law which does not include giving an opinion or carrying a message (p. 307), but he obviously gossips to rich clients because Miss Havisham knows about Pip's great expectations (pp. 184, 373).

His discordant name, brusque manner and burly build project a frightening image. He has a big head – literally and figuratively – balding on top; his big hands with a big bitten, threatening forefinger; his big, bushy, black eyebrows and big 'black dots of beard and whisker'; his big gold watch-chain; his big 'bright creaking boots' – all overpower and intimidate everyone in court including the justices (p. 225) and jury (p. 406). If he needs anything further to petrify a client or witness, his big, silk pocket handkerchief, used at the dramatic moment, adds the finishing touch.

His great expectation is to have his own way, and he first achieves this when he persuades Molly to give up her daughter (p. 425). Her case is the start of his brilliant career and he progresses from one success to another always having his own way, and earning a great reputation for himself.

When Jaggers is 'at it' (p. 224) he bullies everyone in sight, throwing his big bitten forefinger and saying 'I'll have it out of you!' or pouncing on an unfortunate with his triumphant 'Now I have got you!'. This bullying manner does not stop after he leaves court either, and he lords it over everyone as he walks majestically about Little Britain and environs.

As a man he is unlovable and unemotional, except for the one time he smiles, amused at the thought of Wemmick's separate Walworth life (p. 424). If he has any compassion, he does not show it. Take, for example, Mike, a regular client. He is upset when his daughter is arrested for shop-lifting, but Jaggers sends him packing: 'I'll have no feelings here. Get out' (p. 427). Do you not think his attitude to people is summed up in his hideous plaster casts (p. 223), for what kind of person keeps real death-masks in his office to remind him of the gallows and his 'world of credit'?

Such is Jaggers's power that he has no need to lock a door or window. No thief dares cross his threshold. A visitor invited to cross it could sum up his house in the sombre words 'dark brown and dismal'. It is far removed from Wemmick's home and strongly resembles the office, being functional rather than decorative.

Those who move in criminal circles cannot help being contaminated and Jaggers probably regrets that he lives 'in an atmosphere of evil' (p. 424). He can never relax, and he comes automatically to 'put a case' instead of the truth; or to discuss something like Pip's predicament in a roundabout way when he obviously knows what is happening but does not want to be incriminated (p. 350). He cannot even be natural on a social occasion and cross-examines the glass and wine (p. 263) and arrests the trumps (p. 264).

In a brief, unguarded moment one day, after Pip has told Jaggers who Estella's father is (p. 422), something human is released. He starts; and when he smiles about Wemmick, he sighs, too. Does Jaggers sigh for the home he never had? Or for the dreams that did not materialize? Or for having been tainted by prison and crime so long that he cannot wash himself clean?

This is an oft-repeated ritual: he tries to absolve himself with the outward and visible sign of his highly-scented soap, and as he scrubs his dirty hands – and on bad days his face and nails as well – outwardly he is clean, but inwardly the taint of prison and crime can never be washed away.

Jaggers is a key character who holds the three stories together. When Miss Havisham asks him for a child to adopt, he is taking up Molly's case. Saving Estella from a life of possible crime and certain neglect is Jaggers's one positive, redeeming act. He does not know the 'man called Abel' (p. 419), but Magwitch knows him, and when he needs a lawyer Jaggers is the obvious choice. Pip meets Jaggers for the first time at Satis House (p. 111) and hears about Miss Havisham's relations from him (pp. 166, 199). As Jaggers becomes his guardian his misconceptions about his benefactor are inevitable.

## WEMMICK

Wemmick leads a double life. Physically he is a short, middle-aged man not exactly handsome, having a squarish face with pitted skin and small, black 'glittering eyes'. His most prominent feature is his mouth, which resembles the slit in a pillar-box, and through which he posts biscuits and other food, and in which he rests his pen.

He has a less than human London appearance, probably due to the atmosphere in Jaggers's office where he works as a clerk. He is a loyal, conscientious, mechanical employee always praising Jaggers's skill (e.g. pp. 222, 404) but confessing that he feels more relaxed out of his company than in it.

He carries caution to extremes, hiding the safe key down his back 'like an iron pigtail' (p. 222), never naming names of clients (p. 384) nor leaving anything about in writing (p. 428) – not even an anonymous message like 'Don't go home' (pp. 381, 382) which would not have been dangerous even if Compeyson had found it.

Over the years delegated authority has come his way, so that he represents Jaggers with some of the same bearing and, although he is more approachable, the clients know where to draw the line. Life has taught him not to miss an opportunity and his great expectation is to 'get hold of portable property' (p. 224). He has already acquired a considerable collection of mourning rings and seals, many of which he wears on his fingers or watch-chain. The fact that they are gifts from condemned criminals does not worry him at all. In London he is far too insensitive to think about the personal connections. He regards the loss of Magwitch's property as a disaster which could have been averted. The odds had been stacked against the convict ever since Compeyson had been on his trail, but 'portable property' is a different matter. That could have been salvaged (pp. 386, 461). Although he is hard, like the society he lives in, there is a glimmer of something else, as we see in the cells at Newgate, but his concern for the prisoners does not prepare us for the pleasant surprise of meeting John Wemmick at home.

If he is dehumanized at work, he is genuinely human at home. His care for his Aged Parent is touching, and he shows infinite patience making the old gentleman feel wanted and important. Warmth and happiness pervade Walworth, and there is much nodding, smiling, security, buttered toast and cosiness.

Miss Skiffins completes the homely atmosphere and, although Jaggers would never have believed it, Wemmick is in love. He marries Miss Skiffins one day in a perfect little ceremony, beautifully arranged in a village church (p. 463), but because caution has become Wemmick's second nature, he pretends that it has all happened by chance. Everything about him is eccentric but harmless; at least his people are homely, hospitable and honest. His love for the Aged Parent and Mrs Wemmick are real enough, and reminiscent of the true qualities that radiate from Joe's forge.

Pip's first unfavourable impression changes as he gets to know Wemmick better and he has reason to be grateful to him for all kinds of reasons as time passes, not least for his hospitality at Walworth where Pip feels 'snugly cut off' (p. 315) and where he knows he can get Wemmick's genuine advice (p. 314) as opposed to his office opinion (p. 310). He does not like mixing business and pleasure and he keeps his two identities separate, but on one occasion they reveal themselves in Jaggers's office much to Wemmick's embarrassment and Jaggers's amusement.

On that particular day, Pip turns to his good friend in desperation as 'a man with a gentle heart' (p. 423) to speak to Jaggers on his behalf. Wemmick stands up to his superior's taunts well and Pip gets the information he wants.

Some parts of Walworth Castle are sham, some ingenious and others quite ridiculous, but it is Wemmick's home and his response to the colourless London life and the falseness he finds there.

## ESTELLA

The ways of the heart are strange, but Pip's infatuation for Estella seems unlikely. When they first meet, the usual appealing qualities of kindness, humour, unselfishness and concern for someone else arc all painfully lacking. Estella is unkind to the point of causing mental and physical hurt (pp. 92, 111); there is no sign of laughter in her proud eyes (except once); her moods (p. 123) reflect her total selfishness, and she cares nothing for the effect her scornful words have on Pip. Biddy – without even seeing Estella – knows that she is not worth the misery and shame (p. 156) she causes Pip.

Is it feasible that Miss Havisham could exploit her so much that Estella has no control at all over her own life? It makes some sort of sense while she is at Satis House, because a little girl of three from a poor background would be excited by the jewels, fine clothes, and the pretty lady in her wedding-dress. She would love the attention and would not know what was happening to her. Miss Havisham could steal her heart and feelings before she even realized it. Away from home and open to other influences, would that coldness hold?

Pip meets Estella again when they are about eighteen, and the first thing he notices is the same insensitive expression in her eyes. Her beauty is breathtaking, and if it has attracted him before, it compels him now. It is obvious that Estella's life is controlled by Miss Havisham, and the greedy woman hangs on to her treasured possession with an uncanny eagerness. Estella seems to think, as does Pip, that they are intended for each other, and that they are Miss Havisham's puppets, with no choice but to obey her instructions (p. 285). There is neither progress nor happiness in their relationship, and Estella responds without emotion except when she laughs about the Pockets' failure to turn Miss Havisham against Pip (p. 286).

One day Estella begins to take on the appearance of a person with a mind of her own. She stands up to Miss Havisham's accusation that she is 'stock and stone' (p. 322). She is graceful, dignified and calm as she gives matter-of-fact answers to all the charges levelled at her. Analysing her upbringing, she says she is the result of what her 'mother by adoption' has made her. 'I must be taken as I have been made. The success is not mine, the failure is not mine, but the two together make me' (p. 324).

Human nature cannot be stifled indefinitely. In spite of Miss Havisham's brainwashing and in spite of herself, Estella feels something for Pip now and again. This is a paradox, but what other reason can she have had for warning him off so often (e.g. pp. 259, 287, 319)? There are inconsistencies in her character which make a clear-cut picture impossible. If heart and memory are linked, as she once said they might be (p. 259), her heart must feel Pip's outpouring of love when they part, because she remembers some of his words for eleven years. Why then does she marry Drummle? Can it have been to save Pip from a loveless marriage with her? Why bother if she has no feeling for him? We can go round and round in circles trying to make sense of it and still not arrive at a convincing conclusion.

Marriage to Drummle is a drastic way out, except that suffering prepares her for a more hopeful relationship with Pip, and her great expectation must be that they will meet again so that she can tell him that he has often been in her thoughts.

Estella's name suggests that she is beyond reach, and cold like the stars. By the time she has suffered years of misery with Drummle, Estella is ready for Pip's love and friendship.

## HERBERT POCKET

Although Herbert is a natural gentleman, his clothes are shabby and his surroundings rather bare, subtly emphasizing that money and rank are not synonymous. He is about the same age as Pip, a little awkward in manner but with a cheerful, friendly disposition and an optimistic viewpoint. He is always looking about him and his great expectation is that something will turn up so that he can make a career for himself.

He is 'on the lookout for good fortune' when he challenges Pip to a fight in their youth (pp. 119–20) but he does not know then, nor in fact until many years later, that his opponent will help him to realize it (pp. 375, 408–9).

Herbert's family is a constant source of embarrassment as both his parents are inadequate – particularly his mother – and he looks forward to life with Clara, his fiancée, rejoicing significantly in the fact that she has no relations. He does not mind that she is below his 'mother's nonsensical family notions' (pp. 272, 389). It is what she is that matters, and he loves her.

Herbert likes Pip for himself, too, but at Pip's request helps him to learn the ways and manners of a gentleman. He is uncritical and especially kind about it, taking care never to hurt Pip's feelings – the hallmark of true gentility.

They become good friends, exchanging confidences, sharing amenities, rowing, walking and generally enjoying themselves so much so that they inevitably fall into debt. Herbert can ill-afford this, but he lacks the moral courage to call a halt.

He does not flinch, however, when he feels he has to warn Pip against Estella. He can see through the sham of her unnatural life and knows Pip's relationship with her will only lead 'to miserable things' (p. 271).

One joyous afternoon Herbert explains to Pip how his opening has 'come at last' (p. 317). He is thrilled at his prospects and determined to make the most of his opportunities. Pip has come of age, but Herbert has no reason to connect the two events and no idea that he also has a benefactor.

When Magwitch shatters both their lives, Herbert is a staunch friend, offering advice and loyal support and showing sympathetic understanding. For example, he sits in Magwitch's chair, remembers and pushes it aside as a token of his abhorrence on Pip's behalf (p. 356). When Pip breaks down, he pretends not to notice his tears, but Pip feels a warm, reassuring grip on his hand.

Herbert could be forgiven for objecting to his rooms being used by a returned transport, but all he seems concerned about is the convict's effect on his friend. This is another hallmark of gentility – putting others first whatever the cost.

He does it again when Pip is away and Magwitch is in danger. Then he is prepared to put the criminal under the same roof as Clara (p. 384), for Pip's sake, which seems an extraordinary risk to take. He promises 'We'll see it out together, dear old boy' (p. 359) and he is as good as his word – as every true gentleman is.

Herbert is the best sort of friend, aware of Pip's needs and ready to lend a hand whatever the risks. When he leaves for Cairo, there is real warmth in his invitation to Pip to join his firm and home at any time.

## BIDDY

Biddy, 'who was the most obliging of girls' (p. 102), is one of those people who is easily taken for granted. She gives Pip extra tuition (p. 103), moves into the forge to look after Mrs Joe and household (p. 150), and becomes Pip's confidante and friend (p. 154).

Pip notices that her eyes are 'very pretty and very good' and that she has smartened herself up since the days of the Dame School, but whatever her virtues, her commonness cancels them all out. What more can anyone ask than a friend who is 'pleasant, wholesome and sweet-tempered'?

There are few completely unselfish people in the world, but Biddy is one of them. She loves Pip but has sufficient self-respect to change her tears to laughter when he fails to realize it (p. 153). She bears his atrocious condescension with commendable patience, quietly putting in a gentle word here and there to register her disapproval at his artificial ideas about being a gentleman (p. 154f). Biddy is 'the wisest of girls' and knows exactly how to help Pip; they might have made a happy couple without his false notions.

Sadly, however, it is true that familiarity breeds contempt, and during his last week at home, when Biddy tells him a few truths about himself and his attitude to Joe, Pip's contempt is ungentlemanly, to say the least. Biddy is right, but Pip blames her for her 'bad side of human nature' and unjustly accuses her of being jealous about his good fortune (p. 176).

The next time they meet is at Mrs Joe's funeral, but Biddy has written to him once on Joe's behalf. It is a pity she did not go to London with Joe because she would have put Pip in his place, but she could not go with a message from Estella when she was against the falseness of that 'friendship'. She suffers worse behaviour from Pip after the funeral and, because she speaks the truth again about his character weakness, he is more insulting than before (p. 303). She does not go on the Rampage, but quietly hands him milk and bread as he is leaving, and tells him not to be hurt. Hers is true, caring love.

The same kind of love motivates her to teach Joe to read and write. It is not because she wants to improve him, but because she wants him to enjoy the achievement (p. 473).

It is hard to keep calm in the face of behaviour like Pip's, but it is certainly more dignified. Biddy's serenity and wisdom, truth and goodness are worth more than anyone's fortune. She is one of the few characters content to be herself, without great expectations.

Is it inevitable that she should marry Joe, or does it come as a surprise? There are hints at the beginning that Biddy has feelings for Pip (p. 152). We do not think about a relationship between Biddy and Joe during Pip's absence from the forge, because Pip's narration dominates the book. On reflection, though, considering what they have both suffered and shared, the marriage was probably inevitable.

## MRS JOE

Mrs Joe reveals her personality in the caustic way she cuts the bread-and-butter (p. 42). The pins and needles that litter the bib of her coarse apron are further signs of her prickly and unfeminine nature. The redness of her skin makes a child think she has washed with a nutmeg-grater instead of soap.

She makes Pip's life a misery, expecting everlasting gratitude because she has brought him up 'by hand'. She abuses both Pip and Joe, reminding them that she is 'a slave with her apron never off' (p. 53) and often finds compensation for her self-inflicted martyrdom in getting out the dustpan.

Being 'given to government' (p. 79) her great expectation is to have her own way and she goes on the Rampage whenever she feels angry or jealous (e.g. pp. 40, 126). Such is 'the stupendous power of money' that the day after an alarming Rampage she actually laughs – a very rare occurrence – when Joe gives her the twenty-five guineas from Miss Havisham who has indirectly caused all the trouble in the first place.

Mrs Joe represents false values and projects a less than human image because her priorities are all wrong. Instead of loving Pip for himself, she makes him feel a nuisance and a cross that she has to bear. The same goes for Joe, and she does not realize his worth until she has been badly injured and cannot speak properly (p. 302). Once she has been disabled, we feel some sympathy for her.

## PUMBLECHOOK

The corrupting power of wealth has tainted the imposter Pumble-chook. His business is successful and he can afford a chaise-cart – a respectable status symbol – but he is not content to let things rest there. With great expectations of recognition, he has to be someone, so he elects to be head of the Gargery family circle (pp. 63, 133) and an authority on Pip's prospects and progress (pp. 83, 124, 132), ever reminding him to be grateful.

The overbearing, hypocritical character does not fool Pip who sees him for what he is, 'that fearful Impostor' (p. 131). Study Pumble-chook and you will see 'a large, hard-breathing, middle-aged, slow man, with a mouth like a fish, dull staring eyes and sandy hair standing upright . . .', a character ripe for caricature.

He represents the vileness of a society that exploits its weakest members and worships those with wealth. 'What's in it for me?' might be his catch-phrase as he starves a child in need of a meal (p. 84) and feeds the man who is not (pp. 179–82). Count how many times he offers his hand on Pip's new wealth (p. 180f) and notice his condescension when Pip finally loses it all (p. 483).

In Pip's absence, he claims the credit for the boy's rise to fame (p. 252) and later spreads malicious stories of the ingratitude of the same boy of whom he was the earliest benefactor and founder of his fortunes (p. 431). He is Dickens's mockery of a pompous materialist and those 'dull staring eyes' reflects his insensitivity. Pumblechook's ridiculous name suggests his stupidity.

## WOPSLE

Wopsle, a bald-headed man with a Roman nose, has no idea of his limitations and is incapable of facing up to reality. Like Pip, he chases dreams. At first as parish clerk, he believes he is God's gift to the Church and that he can outshine any clergyman given the chance. Puffed up with his own importance, he performs at the Dame School (p. 74), at Pumblechook's (pp. 144–5) and at the Three Jolly

Bargemen, but there he folds up under Jaggers's bullying (p. 160 f).

When he exchanges the Church for the stage, he makes a ludicrous exhibition of himself as Hamlet. It is as impossible for him to be an actor as it is for a blacksmith's boy to be a gentleman: wearing a wig, black cloak and Danish costume does not make a Hamlet any more than mere wealth and education make a gentleman.

'Reviewing his success and developing his plans' (p. 278) does not get Wopsle far. Instead of 'reviving the drama' Pip says he has 'partaken of its decline' (p. 395). He is last seen in a third-rate pantomime. His absurd name conveys the absurd nature of his character.

## ORLICK

Orlick has no saving grace. 'He [is] a broad-shouldered loose-limbed swarthy fellow of great strength, never in a hurry and always slouching' (p. 140). Starved of any kind of relationship, he finds consolation in sinister activities like scaring the child Pip nearly to death (p. 140) and viciously mugging Mrs Joe (pp. 146, 437).

A criminal nature, jealousy, brute force, thwarted passion and years of harbouring grudges lead Orlick to seek his revenge. He blames Pip for his failure and he plans to murder his 'brother' and dispose of his body in the limekiln (p. 436).

Loitering and slouching – always in the shadows – this ruthless villain attracts others of similar inclination and he becomes a spy for Compeyson (p. 438). Finally, he is imprisoned for a relatively minor crime (p. 475), but the fact remains that he represents the basest evil and it is significant that Biddy cannot bear to be anywhere near him (p. 158) and Joe knocks him flat (p. 142).

## COMPEYSON

Compeyson is a refined crook and, although his public-school background gives him more than a head start in court, he is a despicable villain with absolutely nothing to commend him. Even his brilliant brain is put to evil use, and his life is spent wickedly exploiting others – especially Miss Havisham and Magwitch – for the expectation of financial gain.

He is brutal to his wife and has no compassion for the dying Arthur, so we can believe Magwitch when he says Compeyson has 'no more heart than an iron file' and is as 'cold as death'. Had he married Miss Havisham he would have added bigamy to his list of crimes which include fraud, forgery, theft and blackmail.

His 'code' does not even include honour among thieves, for when he turns informer, hoping for a substantial reward (p. 458), he deceives his cronies and that is how Wemmick is misled.

## BENTLEY DRUMMLE

Bentley Drummle's great expectation is a title. He is 'the next heir but one to a baronetcy' (p. 215), but anyone less like a member of the aristocracy would be hard to imagine. He has a feeble brain and is motivated by instinct more akin to a criminal's than a gentleman's, as Jaggers is quick to notice. His loutish figure and unco-ordinated bearing emphasize his lack of intelligence; a sulky disposition rounds off this unpleasant character.

Pip loathes him, and Estella cannot break his heart because he is even more heartless than she is. Drummle respects no one and treats Estella 'with great cruelty' (p. 490). She surely sighs with relief when, having treated his horse in his usual 'blundering, brutal manner', Drummle has a fatal accident.

## MATTHEW AND BELINDA POCKET

Matthew is a natural gentleman who can see through imposters such as Compeyson. He holds firmly to his belief that 'no man who was not a true gentleman at heart, ever was, since the world began, a true gentleman in manner ... no varnish can hide the grain of the wood ...' (p. 204).

His prominent feature is his dishevelled very grey hair which he tugs with both hands (pp. 215–17) in a symbolic effort to extricate himself from his domestic confusion. He wins Pip's respect as a scholar and tutor and, finally, Miss Havisham's recognition of his virtues when she leaves him £4,000 (pp. 205, 374, 474).

Belinda represents the idle rich, being the daughter of a knight, who marries beneath her. She lives an artificial, useless existence as futile as Pip's conception of gentility.

## THE POCKETS (*Sarah, Camilla, Georgiana*)

These Pockets, 'the toadies and humbugs' (p. 109), are Miss Havisham's parasitic relations who feed on the great expectation of inheriting a sizable fortune. They fawn upon Pip to his face (p. 226) and try to destroy him behind his back (p. 286). They flatter Miss Havisham with base ulterior motives, but she has the measure of them and loses no opportunity in letting them believe Pip will be her heir. Sarah grows 'greener and yellower' and their jealousy and love of money destroys them as human beings. They get what they deserve from Miss Havisham (p. 475).

## OTHER CHARACTERS

There are many characters in *Great Expectations* who play minor but important roles. Their first mention in the book is indicated by the chapter numbers in parentheses. Aged Parent (ch. 25); the Avenger (ch. 27); Bill Barley (ch. 46); Clara Barley (ch. 30); Mrs Brandley (ch. 38); Clarriker (ch. 37); Mrs Coiler (ch. 23); Flopson (ch. 22); Pip Gargery (ch. 59); Arthur Havisham (ch. 22); the Hubbles (ch. 4); the Jack (ch. 54); Lazarus (ch. 20); man with the file (ch. 10); Mike (ch. 20); Millers (ch. 22); Molly (ch. 24); the Pockets – Jane, Allick, Baby (ch. 22); Mrs Raymond (ch. 11); Miss Skiffins (ch. 37); Startop (ch. 23); Mr Trabb (ch. 19); Trabb's boy (ch. 19); Mrs Whimple (ch. 46); Wopsle's great-aunt (ch. 7).

# Commentary

## First person narrative

In a first person narrative, everything is seen, heard and experienced through the senses of the narrator. It is an intimate style of writing and the mature Pip takes the reader into his confidence and discusses his strengths and weaknesses with incredible honesty and understanding. He makes no excuses as he examines his motives and we live the same life vicariously.

Other people's stories have to be told when the narrator is present, so one major problem is that in autobiographical writing the reader can never know the thoughts and feelings of the other characters.

## Melodrama

Melodrama is an exaggerated form of writing that spills over into the ludicrous. It originated on the nineteenth-century stage. Characters overacted and indulged in sensational behaviour, depicting one extreme of goodness and the other extreme of evil. When it broke the bounds of reality, no one minded. It added to the enjoyment.

To describe writing as 'melodramatic' in literary criticism means that characters have been released from the constraints of natural behaviour, so that exaggeration, coincidence, and anything farfetched in character or plot can be believed. Thus we accept Miss Havisham's abnormality without querying the possibility of such a life. That is not important. What matters is her role and contribution to the themes. Similarly, we can accept the various coincidences, realizing that they are a legitimate part of the novel's form.

## Irony

Irony is a term regularly used in literary criticism for words that are not literally true and situations that are not exactly what they seem.

For example, just before Pip sets out for London he recalls the convict and comforts himself with the thought that he will not see him again (p. 173). The irony is that his expectations have been provided by the convict's money, and he *will* see him again. When Magwitch looks around 'as if he had some part in the things he admired . . .' (p. 333) of course he has. That too, is irony. The mood of the whole novel is ironical because it hinges on the fact that things and people are not always what they seem.

*Style*

The most striking characteristic of Dickens's writing is its ease of expression, with imagery and symbolism gloriously interwoven. Every emotion, person, place, incident, setting and thing is credible (now that we understand the technique that allows the gross overstatement and coincidence of melodrama), and is the result of keen observation and an exceptional eye for detail.

His characters live in carefully selected surroundings and speak as they have been cast: the bullying Jaggers, the melodramatic Miss Havisham, the free-and-easy Herbert, the uncouth Magwitch, the simple Joe . . .

Dickens moves us to laughter, even tears, with the humour that he has packed into his narrative. He intends Joe to be 'very funny' but sometimes the humour verges on pathos – for example, when Joe is so out of place, clutching his hat like a 'bird's-nest with eggs in it' (p. 241) on his visit to London. Farce, parody, wit, satire and straightforward humour are all included in abundance and the reader should have no difficulty in selecting examples of each kind.

Graphic images of people and places are our lasting memories of Dickens's writing. We shall never forget, for example, the weird Miss Havisham in her great, gruesome house. Dickens appeals to all our senses as he writes, and we can see Joe in his best clothes 'like a scarecrow in good circumstances' (p. 54) and the firework Pip made of the Aged's sausage (p. 382). We taste with him the 'tingling' of the beer (p. 93) and the bad nut flavour of dry-rot (p. 232); we can smell the blackcurrant leaf that Biddy rubbed to pieces – the smell that 'has ever since recalled . . . that evening . . .' (p. 175) and Pumblechook's '. . . breathing sherry and crumbs' (p. 299); we can hear the familiar sounds in the silence of the unfamiliar hotel bedroom – '. . . the closet whispered, the fireplace sighed, the little washing-stand ticked, and one guitar-string played occasionally in the chest of drawers' (p. 380); and we can feel as Pip does 'A gentle pressure on my hand . . . A stronger pressure on my hand,' until our hands are raised with his to the dying Magwitch's lips (p. 470).

These few morsels are intended to whet your appetite. There is something to savour on every page.

It is plain that Charles Dickens was a genius. His writing has provided his readers with food for thought for over a hundred years, and his themes are as relevant today as they ever were. *Great Expectations* explores many truths, including the contrast between the dream and the reality of wealth; the artificiality and the naturalness of gentility; the sham and the genuineness of relationships. All these ideas are intermingled and lead to the conclusion that it is what we are that matters, not what we own or our position in society.

## *The dream and the reality of wealth*

The dream is of a fairy godmother in the shape of Miss Havisham, a magic wand and a ready-made fortune. When Pip hears about his great expectations he says, 'My dream was out; my wild fancy was surpassed by sober reality . . .' (p. 165). He mentions reality but he does not know the meaning of the word yet.

He soon learns 'the stupendous power of money' and is flattered by phoney respect (pp. 177–9) and servility (pp. 179–82). Sudden wealth can, and does, destroy character. In contemporary life fortunes can change people's lives completely – and not always for the better; we can see that an unexpected fortune can knock some people off balance. It often creates more problems than it solves. But who stops to think with a chance of a fortune at his fingertips?

Pip feels immediately different, venerated, in fact, as his 'sacred person passed'. He puts on the appropriate airs and promotes himself above those at home '. . . bestowing . . . a gallon of condescension upon everybody in the village' (p. 173). He ignores 'the plain honest working life . . .' with 'nothing in it to be ashamed of . . .' (p. 159) and the fact that his roots are with Joe. Under the spell of Satis House and his fortune, Pip turns a deaf ear to the voices of reason (Joe's, p. 100, and Biddy's, pp. 154, 156.) He exchanges his job at the forge for a life of leisure, and pulls up his roots without a thought for the obvious consequences. As for Biddy, she is too ordinary for such a grand fellow as he has become. He has given up his 'coarse and common' ways and that means giving up his 'coarse and common' friends, too. He has much to learn about the worth of truly human people, truths he will only learn from bitter experience.

It is not long before Pip is spending recklessly, living in his affluent dream-world and believing in his expectations. He is extravagant, patronizing and foolish (pp. 235, 240, 292) and, as a fool and his money are soon parted, he begins 'to contract a quantity of debt' (pp. 292, 304). But what does it matter? He believes that his donor will arrive in person, and all will be well.

Magwitch has a dream, too. '. . . if I gets liberty and money, I'll make that boy a gentleman!' (p. 337). When he has the chance to earn money, he works for Pip, enduring insults and abuse but comforted by the look that passed between them that Christmas Day on the marshes (p. 69). Sixteen years later, he risks his life to see the gentleman he has made.

This is the moment of 'sober reality' for Pip. The 'taint of prison and crime' has made him what he is. His wealth is the result of a transport's labour. 'O, that he [Magwitch] had never come! That he had left me at the forge –' He remembers that that was the place where he had once expected to win his independence (p. 134). It is too late now. We can all say 'if only we had' or 'if only we hadn't'. The truth is we did not or we did, and we are stuck with the result of our choices.

The reality is that the power of money corrupts, and those who succumb to its magnetic attraction risk losing their worth as human beings. This is illustrated, for example, in Wemmick's Little Britain demeanour, Jaggers's unapproachability, Compeyson's criminal pursuits, Mrs Joe's sudden change of mood (p. 131), Pumblechook's 'May I?' and Miss Havisham's hold over her greedy relations.

All the fortune does for Pip is to suffocate his better nature and dehumanize him almost to the point of no return. 'Joe . . . the blacksmith . . . sticking to the old work . . .' cannot be contaminated by its power (pp. 168, 481).

Once Magwitch recovers from his initial disappointment and, later, Pip's repugnance has 'all melted away' he and Pip bring out the best in each other as they face 'sober reality' together (pp. 456–70). Ironically neither has any wealth by then!

## The artificiality and the naturalness of gentility

The Victorians believed that people had their appointed places (you will have noticed several references to 'high' and 'low' throughout the novel) and it was a system that bred snobs and social climbers. That is why Pip is so dissatisfied with his lot once Estella has introduced him to artificial values. His dream is to get away from it all: ' "Biddy," said I, after binding her to secrecy, "I want to be a gentleman." ' (p. 154).

If you ask half a dozen people to give you a definition of a gentleman, it is likely that you will have half a dozen different answers. There is the dictionary definition, of course, but that is not quite what we are after in defining the term for the purpose of this novel. For Pip, 'gentleman' is a word that conjures up another world, something beyond his experience but something that sounds fascinating, like the 'young Knight of romance' who marries the 'princess' (p. 253). Herbert quotes Matthew's splendid definition (p. 204) which takes some beating.

The idea of a gentleman is important in *Great Expectations*, and is discussed by Angus Calder in his Introduction (pp. 23, 27). Add, too, some inner attributes and we can say that a gentleman values truth, loyalty, courtesy, patience, gentleness and integrity – like the knights of old that Pip has in mind, or like his friend, Herbert. Herbert has natural appeal and the manners and values of a true gentleman. His caring attitude and true chivalry are apparent throughout the novel (e.g. pp. 201 f, 243, 248, 268 f, 277, 292 f, 355 f, 384, 388 f, 416 f, 428, 441, 452, 459, 489). This is the vital truth which Pip fails to grasp at the beginning – that a gentleman acts naturally and has no need to pretend. Joe can see it, though. He sums it up when he tells Biddy, 'Pip's a gentleman of fortun', then' (p. 170); that is, one who pretends to be a gentleman or, in other words, an imposter. This blacksmith has a rare knack of arriving at the exact conclusion.

This is born of patient observation and it is not unusual to find the simplest folk are the wisest. Joe accepts himself as he is and knows the artificiality of putting on different clothes and pretending to be someone else (pp. 54, 127, 246, 301). He knows the comfort of familiar surroundings (p. 246) and advises Pip to 'keep company with common ones' (p. 100). Biddy, too, has the same natural standards. She respects and accepts Joe as he is. Unlike Pip, she sees no need to 'improve' him – nor do we.

They both love Pip for himself and grieve to see him acting out of character. Natural gentility does not bear grudges or make possessive demands, so when Pip is ready he is welcomed back, with open arms. No one says, 'I told you so!' – just that he has made their day complete (p. 487). This is the sacrificial love that only the unpretentious can give. Pip learns this when he is able to say to Magwitch, 'I will be as true to you as you have been to me!' (p. 457).

Wealth, material possessions, education – all the outward signs of gentility that Estella had made him hanker after – are false attributes. Gentility is none of these things. It is elusive and comes when it is least expected. Once Pip recognizes in Joe 'a gentle Christian man' (p. 472) and the futility of his own artificial idea of a gentleman, he becomes 'a gentleman at heart'.

### The sham and the genuineness of relationships

Using people as a means to an end like instruments or tools is exploitation. Those who exploit others are often less than human and capable of causing distress, serious enough to wreck their victims' lives. This is clear all through *Great Expectations*.

Take Miss Havisham as an example. Her name gives the clue to her false relationships. In her raving for revenge she values that above all else. She does not stop to think what she is doing to Estella. She works on the 'impressionable child' with praises, jewels, teachings, and the broken figure of herself always there as a warning to illustrate the lessons, until Estella's heart is as cold as ice (p. 412). Deprived of all natural influences and drained of all natural feeling,

Estella becomes a performing puppet trained to break men's hearts.

Just look at the effect this has on them both: they are unnatural. Miss Havisham is degraded and lacking in self-respect; Estella is heartless and unable to respond to people as a woman.

Miss Havisham's exploitation does not stop here. Through Estella she affects several others including Pip, who becomes a victim – and, indirectly, Joe does, too. It is her influence that leads Pip into his world of false dreams and false hopes which almost ruins his life and certainly destroys his best years. 'Love her, love her, love her! How does she use you?' asks the scheming woman with 'passionate eagerness' (p. 261).

Pip is made a convenience of at Satis House to torment the Pockets and provide Estella with a model on which to practise (p. 341). He knows that he and Estella are Miss Havisham's puppets (p. 288) and that he is being used (p. 318), but he cannot help himself. Such is Miss Havisham's domination.

'No man is an Island, entire of it self' we are told. Whatever we do touches those around us. Inevitably, Joe is caught in Miss Havisham's trap. Pip's infatuation for Estella dominates his thinking, and when he first hears about his great expectations, and that he must leave for London, he is sure that he will one day be in a position to marry her. He does not think about the effect on Joe.

Suddenly the blacksmith's world is in ruins (no more 'what larks' or 'Pip, old chap' but 'Sir' or 'Pip or Sir') but Joe, unlike most of us, bears it. '. . . Joe never complained of anything . . . but ever did his duty in his way of life, with a strong hand, a quiet tongue, and a gentle heart' (p. 303). So much does Pip abuse him, it is a wonder his heart does not break. He is finally rewarded when Pip comes to his senses, acknowledges the worth of all that Joe stands for, and honours Joe and Biddy because they are 'both so good and true' (p. 488).

Dickens felt deeply about wealth and class and exploitation of every kind, and he criticized the resulting social ills in his writing. In Magwitch, he has created a character who is forced into a life of crime by conditions over which he has no control – poverty, ignorance, insecurity. Society makes him an outcast, but he gets his own back and buys a gentleman better than any who had a hand in his downfall. Judging by his ability to do this and the way he behaves once he knows the warmth of mattering to somebody, we cannot help wondering what kind of life Magwitch might have had. In his ignorance, he does not realize that so much wealth will turn a village lad's head.

Pip becomes Magwitch's victim, and so it is that 'the taint of prison and crime' haunts him throughout his adventures, until the final irony when he discovers that all his pretensions have been in vain.

In his search for the crock of gold, Pip sees only the rainbow. But he cannot find where it ends. While he chases after it he is blind and deaf to the truth around him. By the time he has realized that no man finds the rainbow's end and the crock of gold is an illusion, it is too late, and he has 'lost all he once hoped for' (p. 481).

But he has at least found himself. At last he knows that things of the truest worth demand a higher price than money, and that it is not until we have made some sacrifices for others that love, forgiveness, freedom and self-respect are within reach. Miracles happen and a little love works wonders. In contrast to the falseness of the Miss Havisham–Estella relationship, the Magwitch–Pip one develops into something genuine.

There is hope, too, for Pip and Estella now they have learnt from their mistakes and their suffering (p. 493). As the evening mists rise, the expectation is that tomorrow will be a greater day.

# Glossary

*Accoucheur policeman:* a policeman at the bedside; Pip suggests he was arrested for the crime of being born

*Apostrophe:* an address to someone (often absent or dead) as though he were there

*Beggar my neighbour:* card game

*Biling:* boiling

*Blacking:* boot polish, made from a mixture of finely-ground animal charcoal, sulphuric acid, vinegar and molasses

*Blade:* dashing young man

*Bound:* legally signed the indentures

*Buster:* slang for one who destroys

*By hand:* bottle fed

*Clicked:* sound of emotion

*Cool:* unexaggerated

*Cove:* slang for fellow

*Doo:* due

*Drawd:* drawn

*Ekerval:* equal

*Ekervally partickler:* equally particular

*Farden:* farthing; coin of little worth

*Gay:* merry

*Grubber:* from grub, slang for food

*Heaped ... head:* Joe returns Pip's unkindness with kindness and thus makes him ashamed

*Hercules:* outstanding quality

*Hout:* (Joe's) out!

*In sunders:* asunder

*Intercourse:* communication, conversation

*Iron:* ankle ring

*Kind of loops:* hangman's

*Meshes:* marshes

*Metaphysics:* (a case of) what comes first

*Mogul:* tyrant

*National Bard:* Shakespeare

*National Debt:* the vast sum owed by the government to individuals and foreign governments

*Nevvy:* nephew

*Obligated:* obliged

*Oncommon:* genteel

*Outdacious:* audacious

*Plaister:* poultice

*Post-office:* metaphor, making an indirect comparison between the shape of Wemmick's mouth and the slit in a pillar-box

*Purple leptic:* apoplectic

*Ram-paged out:* rushed out angrily

*Rich man:* Jesus said it was impossible for a rich man to enter God's Kingdom because he could not resist temptation

*Roman nose:* nose with a high bridge

*Sumever:* soever

*Taken down:* removed from the gallows

*Tap:* short for taproom, a bar

*Tartar:* spiteful woman

*Tar-water:* a medicine of water and tar taken to cure indigestion

*Tremenjous:* tremendous

*Vicariously:* experienced at second hand by sympathetic sharing of another's experiences

*Warmint:* varmint (from vermin); nuisance

*Whatsume'er:* whatsoever

*Witches' caldron:* reference to the apparitions that the witches raised for Macbeth from their caldron

*Wittles:* food

# Examination Questions

1. Either (*a*) Describe Pip's first meeting with Herbert Pocket, and explain why he later had reason to be grateful for his friendship.

Or (*b*) Show how Dickens gives vivid descriptions of the sad, comic, and strange sides of London life in the nineteenth century.

(*Associated Examining Board*)

2. Either (*a*) Do you find Jaggers a likeable character? Give your reasons, supporting them with illustrations from the novel.

Or (*b*) Illustrate by close reference to the novel the remark that 'in *Great Expectations* there is justice for the rich but none for the poor'.

(*Associated Examining Board*)

3. Either (*a*) What does the character of Miss Havisham add to the atmosphere of the novel and the intrigue of the plot?

Or (*b*) For what reasons should Pip have felt a great debt of gratitude to Joe Gargery?

(*Associated Examining Board*)

4. Either (*a*) Consider the sequence of events at the opening of the novel (from Pip's first encounter with Magwitch until the latter is recaptured for the first time) and discuss (i) Dickens's ability to create an atmosphere of tension and fear; and (ii) why these events may be said to be the key to the plot of the novel.

Or (*b*) Discuss the author's skill in creating grotesque or fantastic characters by reference to two of the characters in this novel.

(*Associated Examining Board*)

5. Either (*a*) Why is the character of Compeyson important to the plot of the novel?

Or (*b*) 'Pip discovers, during the course of the novel, what are the really important things in life.' Do you agree? Support your opinion by close reference to the novel.

(*Associated Examining Board*)

6. 'As a boy, Pip had an eventful and difficult life.' Do you agree?
(*Southern Universities Joint Board*)

7. Dickens's skill is especially prominent in his creation of Magwitch. Discuss the convict's importance, both as a key figure in Pip's life, and as a means of criticizing society.

(*Southern Universities Joint Board*)

8. 'Dickens's most grotesque characters are often his most vivid.' Discuss, with reference to *two* of: Pumblechook; Trabb's Boy; Orlick.

(*Southern Universities Joint Board*)

9. Compare and contrast the two 'lives' of Wemmick.
(*Southern Universities Joint Board*)

10. 'Estella is a truly tragic character.' Discuss.
(*Southern Universities Joint Board*)

11. 'Throughout the story Dickens never lets us forget that danger and evil are everywhere.' Is this tenable?
(*Southern Universities Joint Board*)

12. What does Dickens's use of Pip as the narrator contribute to our enjoyment of the novel?

(*Southern Universities Joint Board*)

13. Read the following passage, and answer all the questions printed beneath it:

My convict never looked at me, except that once. While we stood in the hut, he stood before the fire looking thoughtfully at it, or putting up his feet by turns upon the hob, and looking thoughtfully at them as if he pitied them for their recent adventures. Suddenly, he turned to the sergeant, and remarked:

'I wish to say something respecting this escape. It may prevent some persons laying under suspicion alonger me.'

'You can say what you like,' returned the sergeant, standing coolly looking at him with his arms folded, 'but you have no call to say it here. You'll have opportunity enough to say about it, and hear about it, before it's done with, you know.'

'I know, but this is another pint, a separate matter. A man can't starve; at least *I* can't. I took some wittles, up at the village over yonder – where the church stands a'most out on the marshes.'

'You mean stole,' said the sergeant.

'And I'll tell you where from. From the blacksmith's.'

'Halloa!' said the sergeant, staring at Joe.

'Halloa, Pip!' said Joe, staring at me.

'It was some broken wittles – that's what it was – and a dram of liquor, and a pie.'

'Have you happened to miss such an article as a pie, blacksmith?' asked the sergeant, confidentially.

'My wife did, at the very moment when you came in. Don't you know, Pip?'

'So,' said my convict, turning his eyes on Joe in a moody manner, and without the least glance at me; 'so you're the blacksmith, are you? Then I'm sorry to say, I've eat your pie.'

'God knows you're welcome to it – so far as it was ever mine,' returned Joe, with a saving remembrance of Mrs Joe. 'We don't know what you have done, but we wouldn't have you starved to death for it, poor miserable fellow-creatur – Would us, Pip?'

The something that I had noticed before, clicked in the man's throat again, and he turned his back.

(i) What had Pip attempted to convey when the convict looked at him *that once* (line 1), and how had he done so?          [4]

(ii) How had the convict acquired the *wittles* (line 13)? How had the theft of the *dram of liquor* (lines 19–20) been concealed, and with what humorous results?          [6]

(iii) *Poor miserable fellow-creatur* (line 31): how far do the

circumstances in which the convict was captured, and his behaviour in this passage, awaken your sympathy for him?          [10]
(*Oxford Local Examinations*)

14. Read the following passage, and answer all the questions printed beneath it:

On the stairs I encountered Wemmick, who was coming down, after an unsuccessful application of his knuckles to my door. I had not seen him alone, since the disastrous issue of the attempted flight; and he had come, in his private and personal capacity, to say a few words of explanation in reference to that failure.

'The late Compeyson,' said Wemmick, 'had by little and little got at the bottom of half of the regular business now transacted, and it was from the talk of some of his people in trouble (some of his people being always in trouble) that I heard what I did. I kept my ears open, seeming to have them shut, until I heard that he was absent, and I thought that would be the best time for making the attempt. I can only suppose now, that it was a part of his policy, as a very clever man, habitually to deceive his own instruments. You don't blame me, I hope, Mr Pip? I am sure I tried to serve you, with all my heart.'

'I am as sure of that, Wemmick, as you can be, and I thank you most earnestly for all your interest and friendship.'

'Thank you, thank you very much. It's a bad job,' said Wemmick, scratching his head, 'and I assure you I haven't been so cut up for a long time. What I look at is, the sacrifice of so much portable property. Dear me!'

'What *I* think of, Wemmick, is the poor owner of the property.'

'Yes, to be sure,' said Wemmick. 'Of course there can be no objection to your being sorry for him, and I'd put down a five-pound note myself to get him out of it. But what I look at, is this. The late Compeyson having been beforehand with him in intelligence of his return, and being so determined to bring him to book, I do not think he could have been saved. Whereas, the portable property certainly could have been saved. That's the difference between the property and the owner, don't you see?'

I invited Wemmick to come up-stairs, and refresh himself with a glass of grog before walking to Walworth.

(i) What is the meaning of *an unsuccessful application of his knuckles to my door* (line 2)? [2]

(ii) Describe *the disastrous issue of the attempted flight* (line 3). [8]

(iii) What do you learn about Wemmick from this passage? [10]

15. Either (*a*) Write an account of Pip's first meeting with Herbert Pocket and show what benefit each derived from their subsequent friendship.

Or (*b*) With reference to any two places presented in *Great Expectations*, illustrate Dickens's ability to make us feel the atmosphere of these places.

(*Oxford Local Examinations*)

# FOR THE BEST IN PAPERBACKS, LOOK FOR THE

In every corner of the world, on every subject under the sun, Penguin represents quality and variety – the very best in publishing today.

For complete information about books available from Penguin – including Pelicans, Puffins, Peregrines and Penguin Classics – and how to order them, write to us at the appropriate address below. Please note that for copyright reasons the selection of books varies from country to country.

---

**In the United Kingdom:** For a complete list of books available from Penguin in the U.K., please write to *Dept E.P., Penguin Books Ltd, Harmondsworth, Middlesex, UB7 0DA*

**In the United States:** For a complete list of books available from Penguin in the U.S., please write to *Dept BA, Penguin, 299 Murray Hill Parkway, East Rutherford, New Jersey 07073*

**In Canada:** For a complete list of books available from Penguin in Canada, please write to *Penguin Books Canada Ltd, 2801 John Street, Markham, Ontario L3R 1B4*

**In Australia:** For a complete list of books available from Penguin in Australia, please write to the *Marketing Department, Penguin Books Australia Ltd, P.O. Box 257, Ringwood, Victoria 3134*

**In New Zealand:** For a complete list of books available from Penguin in New Zealand, please write to the *Marketing Department, Penguin Books (NZ) Ltd, Private Bag, Takapuna, Auckland 9*

**In India:** For a complete list of books available from Penguin, please write to *Penguin Overseas Ltd, 706 Eros Apartments, 56 Nehru Place, New Delhi, 110019*

**In Holland:** For a complete list of books available from Penguin in Holland, please write to *Penguin Books Nederland B.V., Postbus 195, NL–1380AD Weesp, Netherlands*

**In Germany:** For a complete list of books available from Penguin, please write to *Penguin Books Ltd, Friedrichstrasse 10 – 12, D–6000 Frankfurt Main 1, Federal Republic of Germany*

**In Spain:** For a complete list of books available from Penguin in Spain, please write to *Longman Penguin España, Calle San Nicolas 15, E–28013 Madrid, Spain*

## FOR THE BEST IN PAPERBACKS, LOOK FOR THE

## PENGUIN PASSNOTES

This comprehensive series, designed to help O-level and CSE students, includes:

**SUBJECTS**
Biology
Chemistry
Economics
English Language
French
Geography
Human Biology
Mathematics
Modern Mathematics
Modern World History
Narrative Poems
Physics

**SHAKESPEARE**
As You Like It
Henry IV, Part I
Henry V
Julius Caesar
Macbeth
The Merchant of Venice
A Midsummer Night's Dream
Romeo and Juliet
Twelfth Night

**LITERATURE**
Arms and the Man
Cider With Rosie
Great Expectations
Jane Eyre
Kes
Lord of the Flies
A Man for All Seasons
The Mayor of Casterbridge
My Family and Other Animals
Pride and Prejudice
The Prologue to The Canterbury
    Tales
Pygmalion
Saint Joan
She Stoops to Conquer
Silas Marner
To Kill a Mockingbird
War of the Worlds
The Woman in White
Wuthering Heights

# How To Buy An Engagement Ring

## ALASTAIR SMITH

ISBN: 1502319365
ISBN-13: 978-1502319364